McPHEE GRIBBLE/PENGUIN BOOKS

Ann M[illegible] Syd-
ney. Af[illegible] d for
several [illegible] ards/
Radiop[illegible] Don-
ald Ma[illegible] fteen
years, w[illegible] they
moved to Canberra and Ann later returned to library work with the public service. She retired in 1978 and now lives in Sydney. This is her first book.

SOFTLY MY GRIEF

Ann MacDonald

McPHEE GRIBBLE/PENGUIN BOOKS

McPhee Gribble Publishers Pty Ltd
66 Cecil Street
Fitzroy, Victoria, 3065, Australia

Penguin Books Australia Ltd,
487 Maroondah Highway, P.O. Box 257
Ringwood, Victoria, 3134, Australia
Penguin Books Ltd,
Harmondsworth, Middlesex, England
Penguin Books,
40 West 23rd Street, New York, N.Y. 10010, U.S.A.
Penguin Books Canada Ltd,
2801 John Street, Markham, Ontario, Canada L3R 1B4
Penguin Books (N.Z.) Ltd,
182-190 Wairau Road, Auckland 10, New Zealand

First published by McPhee Gribble Publishers
in association with Penguin Books Australia 1988

Typeset in Sabon by Bookset, Melbourne
Made and printed in Australia by
Australian Print Group

National Library of Australia
Cataloguing-in-Publication data
MacDonald, Ann.
Softly my grief.
ISBN 0 14 011592 7.
1. MacDonald, Ann. 2. Women – Australia – Biography. I. Title.
920.72'0994

An earlier version of *Softly My Grief* was published under the title of *Widow*, by Rigby Publishers Ltd, 1981.

McPhee Gribble's creative writing programme is assisted by the Literature Board of the Australia Council.

Beloved,
on that wisp of cloud
two fireflies meet
to spend eternity.
No matter that nature decrees
that it is only momentary
for them this infinitely tiny time
is everlasting.

Anne Parratt

Acknowledgements

The author wishes to thank Anne Parratt for permission to reproduce a verse from her poem 'Empyrean'; George Allen & Unwin for permission to quote from *Lord of the Rings* by J. R. R. Tolkien; and to J. M. Dent & Sons and Dylan Thomas for permission to quote the last verse of 'Do Not Go Gentle Into That Good Night', published in *Dylan Thomas: Collected Poems from 1934 to 1952*.

I

• *November 1976* •
Canberra

A fly buzzes monotonously at the window pane. My love stares fixedly ahead at a future that no longer exists for him. The lines on his face are not carved by bitterness . . . nor even pain . . . just despair, blank, empty, hopeless despair.

'We won't let him suffer,' they said, and they were true to their promise. But who can measure the pain that surges into a man's heart when he finally knows that his battle with an early death is lost – indeed, that it's almost over? Waiting, just waiting, day after day, for the inevitable to happen. Who is to say which is the greater agony – the pain of the flesh being relentlessly consumed by the advancing cancerous cells, or the anguish of the mind forced to relinquish all hold on the future?

'Death is not final . . . it is but the beginning of an even greater existence than anyone can experience on earth.' Ah, but who knows this to be true? Show me one single living creature in this whole universe, who actually knows that death is not just a great emptiness – a pure nothing.

God knows, we both want to believe the chaplain's comforting words. We desperately want to allow his claims to go unchallenged. But as the time of separation comes closer, we both feel the cold, clammy hand of doubt gripping us.

We have ceased to communicate with one another. Words are exchanged, but they are meaningless and without warmth. The only words with any meaning now are 'hullo,' because this means that we are together for yet a little while longer, and 'goodbye' for that may be the last word we ever exchange. The appointment has been made, but the time has not yet been set.

Will his death sneak up surreptitiously and snatch him suddenly when he is alone and unprepared? Or will it stifle his life slowly and agonizingly? I have asked this question repeatedly, knowing full well that no one can tell me the answer. But I still struggle to know. As a last act of love, I want to hold him and comfort him as he leaves this world behind.

II
Days of Happiness

• *1953* •
Christchurch, New Zealand

I went to New Zealand for an extended holiday but soon ran out of funds. Moping around the city wondering what on earth I could do, I passed a large city bookshop and an alarm went off in my brain. I was a librarian. Surely, I could sell books.

The manager wasn't greatly impressed but agreed to try me out. I wasn't very good at the money part but I was good at selling books.

Company policy insisted that staff must always look busy. This meant that if you were not actually serving a customer, you were expected to take a duster and bang two books together and dust the shelves.

One morning I was standing at the top of my ladder in a grey cotton dress and sheer red stockings, banging the books and dusting, when a male voice at the level of my ankles said, 'You know, if you worked in the British Museum Library you would be sacked for treating the books like that.'

Barely controlling my rage, I climbed down the ladder and confronted the arrogant stranger. His smiling blue eyes looked down into mine and I was gone. Well . . . not quite. First, I put him straight on a few points. I explained that I knew a lot more about libraries than he did and probably a great deal more about books.

And thus began a conversation that continued for twenty-four wonderful years.

• *20 March 1954* •
Hunters Hill, N.S.W.

This was the most beautiful day in the world. This was the day we went to the little stone church and promised to love one another for as long as we both should live. My memory is of a peaceful sunny day, bubbling over with quiet happiness.

As the congregation sang

'Frail as summer's flower we flourish . . .'

I looked up at the reassuringly tall, healthy figure beside me and smiled softly.

'. . . Blows the wind and it is gone . . .'

A sudden chill gripped me as I tried to imagine life without him.

Then the music changed, and we moved on further into the lovely afternoon.

• *1955* •

The gentle love of early marriage: the exquisite tenderness of caressing and caring for each other; the passionate sharing of our physical selves. Everything was young and fresh. Each experience had a shiny newness. You, being an only child, found never-ending interest in all things female, be they my clothes, my thoughts, or my enthusiasms, while I sensed with wonder the prospect of imminent motherhood.

Of course, she was bound to be the most beautiful baby in the nursery!

And you didn't really want a PhD anyway. Or did you? I have often wondered. Did you really feel the new-born life was more precious than a PhD? If you didn't, you were extremely good at concealing the fact. It seemed to be as natural to you as breathing, to accept that we were now a family and that your education and my working days were over.

Laughingly, you accepted that I was no Martha and agreed that I was born to be a Mary who would do the flowers and stoke the fire, in preference to scrubbing floors or darning socks. In fact, you finally bowed to the inevitable and darned your own socks.

• *1962* •

New Plymouth, New Zealand

In time, we had three children, two little girls, Sue and Maren, and a baby son called Graeme. We all read a lot and laughed a lot, and were devoted to teddy bears. We lived in a sunny house with a large, messy garden.

For the children, growing up in New Plymouth meant thick, golden gorse bushes that towered over their heads. Over the back fence, horses roamed and sheep grazed quietly on the hills. A penny a bucket was the going rate for manure collected for the garden. It was hard, smelly work, but pennies were hard to come by.

One hot, breathless afternoon a little four-year-old girl packed her doll's clothes and ran away from home. I watched from the kitchen window as she stood halfway down the drive, with a suitcase in one hand and her doll in the other, mutinously kicking a fence post. It wasn't really worth it, not even to make me feel sorry.

Growing up in New Plymouth was playing in fierce, scorching black sand, with the snow-covered peak of Mount Egmont, looming behind; sunny days in the water, snowy days on the mountain; a hammock swinging in the black wattle and the ginger cat watching the little white mouse through the glass on the top of his cage; the sun making patterns on the carpet and the peace of total darkness at night.

In the evening, the flames were reflected in the lovely old brass fender in front of the open fireplace as we read stories. Together, we explored the world of myth, legend and fairy tale, creating our own magic world.

Swimming in the river. Picnic on the rocks. Small children squealing. Tall father watching carefully, enjoying the play with his active young family.

But where's the mother? Where indeed? Well, you see that lady sitting on a rock way up stream, staring dreamily at the trees? That's the mother. She has turned her back on the family and is pretending they don't exist.

Donald, sensing my need to be single for a while, understood perfectly that I would come back to them refreshed and renewed and ready to join in and be a mother again.

• *1964* •

New Plymouth was a very cold, wet part of New Zealand. Raincoats and gumboots were the order of the day throughout most of the winter.

Being a concerned mum, doing what I could to help the children through life as smoothly as possible, I thought about the confusion in the school cloakroom at the end of the day. I realized it must be very difficult for small children to recognize their own black gumboots in a row of some thirty identical pairs.

Then I had what I believed to be a brilliant idea. I got out a pot of bright red paint and painted a large 'M' on the front of each little boot. 'That should do it,' I mused, as I viewed my handiwork with satisfaction. Well, no one else felt quite like that. The children were appalled when they saw what the next rainy day held in store for them. I can still see the dejected little trio, setting off down the drive, too humiliated to even talk to one another. Even now, they still tell friends, 'Do you know our mother once painted enormous red 'M's' on the front of our gumboots!'

School holidays. Constant rain. Restless children.

We decided to make a huge collage. We were going to paint a picture of a fishing village in the Mediterranean.

To avoid argument, each child took responsibility for a particular area. Sue drew all the fishermen at the edge of the water, complete with matchstick rods and nylon lines. Graeme, whose engine was only switched off when he was asleep, drew all the cars and trucks in the street. And Maren, who was a real homebody, drew the houses in the background.

Layer by layer, they built it up. We all made trees and sailing boats and a man sold balloons on the wharf. As a final touch, we teased cotton wool and glued clouds in the sky.

It was a fabulous picture and the holidays passed before we knew it.

• *1969* •

Change was in the air. The girls were about to go to High School and Donald and I were feeling restless. He had been teaching for more than twelve years and was longing to move into planning and administration where he felt new ideas could be implemented.

So we sold the house in New Zealand and moved family, furniture and marmalade cat to Australia. We arrived in January in the midst of a breathless summer.

It was late at night when our plane landed. As we stepped on to the tarmac, Donald took a deep breath of the heavy night air and said 'Mmmmmmmmm . . . this is what I came back for. I do love this country of yours.'

We had planned to settle in Sydney, but shortly after we arrived, Donald was offered a job with the Commonwealth Government in Canberra.

The marmalade cat sat in her basket in the back of the car and yelled all the way from Sydney. He of the quick temper and fiery spirit nearly gave her to the vet in Liverpool.

Long before we reached the national capital, we could see its lights reflected in the night sky. As we drove over Commonwealth Avenue Bridge we wondered what this city held for each of us.

• *1970* •
Canberra

Surprisingly soon we mastered the concentric circles of the road system and bought a block of land with a huge tree on it.

We built a romantic two-storey house with a secluded courtyard and room for a hammock. It was *Anne's House of Dreams* and *The Secret Garden* all rolled into one.

We bought a golden labrador puppy and called her Georgie and our circle was complete.

• *1972* •

The children embraced their adolescence with an enthusiasm that left us breathless. Teenage traumas often fractured the smooth pattern of our existence. All their lives they had been taught to think for themselves and now they did.

Sometimes, we felt too old for parenthood. One weekend, we considered running away from home ourselves.

With Donald well established in his job and everyone else at school, I began to yearn for a greater challenge than the morning coffee round in the suburbs.

As a change from traditional library work, I applied for a job in the Department of Health running an information section on therapeutic drugs. It was a back-up service for the drug evaluators who were concerned with new drugs, adverse effects and congenital abnormalities caused by therapeutic substances. I soon found myself involved in a totally new area that I found stimulating and challenging.

Donald was delighted with my steps towards a life and career of my own. He watched with pride as I became absorbed in a new role and a new pattern of living. Without missing a beat, he shared the cooking and helped organize the housework so that I was free to follow a path of my own choosing. A calm richness and serenity settled on our marriage . . .

. . . until May 1975.

III
The First Symptoms

• *May 1975* •

You presented to your friendly local GP with rectal bleeding, diarrhoea, and vague abdominal discomfort.

'I probably have cancer of the rectum,' you announced cheerfully. 'It's such an inconvenient bloody disease, that it would be just my luck.'

'Mmmm, well, we'll have to see about that, won't we?' he replied.

The examination was painful, but the doctor could see nothing wrong . . . possibly a slight tendency to haemorrhoids. However, being a cautious man, he sent you for a barium enema which showed nothing. With hindsight, an expert was able to detect a slight irregularity that did in fact prove to be the embryo tumour.

Kaomagma and its variants became an integral part of your daily diet.

• *September 1975* •

Still not suspecting any problem, we ran away. For three glorious weeks we ran away from everything and everyone. We paused in Sydney long enough to look at the shops and the galleries. We leaned out the window of our motel and watched the life on the harbour chug past. We dined in exotic places and went to a concert at the Opera House and drowned ourselves in the magic of the harbour lights.

Then we drove north, feeling incredibly young and free

and happy. This was the first holiday we had spent alone for many, many years. We drove along the coast until we came to a beach that invited us to linger awhile and tell of our love. It was stupendous – the sun and the sand and the fragrance of your skin close to mine.

We talked about nothing and about everything. We planned a holiday in the Greek islands for the following May. We thought of the long, beautiful years that lay ahead of us, free from the responsibility of rearing our children. Unambitious in the conventional sense we dreamt of having half a job each, and time, all the time in the world to be together and do all the things we had always wanted to do.

We wandered hand in hand through the old cemetery, blissfully unconscious of our own mortality. We were wonderfully happy and so unaware of the storm clouds gathering.

If you ever happen upon a little ghost wandering along the beach, humming softly to herself and dabbling in the rock pools, leave her be. Don't warn her of the tragedy that lies ahead.

• *9 February 1976* •

Countdown had begun. Until now you had paid spasmodic visits to your GP seeking relief from abdominal discomfort. But this was the day you paid the first of many visits, complaining of fierce, unremitting pain and continual bleeding.

The twentieth of March, our twenty-second wedding anniversary, passed unnoticed in a haze of misery and pain. I think it was only then that real panic took hold of me.

• *24 March* •

This morning I was anxious and withdrawn and found it hard to concentrate on my work. You had done the unbelievable and taken a 'sickie'. One of my medical colleagues sensed my preoccupation and asked if anything was wrong. I described your upset tummy and the steps being taken to relieve it. He lost no time in calling around to see you and arranging for urgent admission to hospital, under the care of his friend, Phillip.

A tentative diagnosis was made within hours. This was followed by several days of tests that appeared to confirm the magnitude of the initial diagnostic error. At this stage, we hoped and expected that the tumour had not spread. The following Tuesday was set for a transverse colon resection.

• *26 March* •

Tonight I was standing at the sweets counter in David Jones, when a voice beside me said, 'Oh, Mrs MacDonald, I have been trying to ring you all this week.' It was our friendly, local GP.

'I had a strange letter from a Dr B. saying that he had admitted your husband to hospital. What happened?' He gathered up his chocolates from the counter.

'He's probably dying,' I whispered.

'Good heavens, I didn't think it was anything serious. Well look, if there's anything I can do . . .'

'No, there's nothing you can do.'

As I turned away, I caught sight of a reflection in a long mirror. Was it me? Was that gaunt, grey-faced old lady really me?

You were able to come home for the weekend, prior to surgery. We made love with a desperation and thoroughness that we had never experienced before. It had never been necessary. Previously, our loving had encompassed all eternity. Therein lay the beauty of it. It would go on forever and gently fade away as we grew old and died. Now fate had interrupted and said harshly, 'You had better get on with your loving. Hurry up. You haven't got forever.'

The intensity and frustration of this kind of lovemaking was new to us both, and we lay back tearful and exhausted, denied the warm glow of soft sleep that normally followed. This was only the beginning, the first frightened step, in our understanding of the way that lay ahead.

Apart from our absolute conviction that we should share our feelings and try to understand our mutual and our separate problems, we had little preparation for such a disaster. Phillip, who was now in charge of all therapy, had stressed the value of sharing our thoughts and concerns, and we knew instinctively that he was right.

Even so, sometimes when you described to me the tests and the assaults on your dignity and humanity, my whole being screamed out inside me. I wanted you to stop torturing me, by describing your torture to me. But I remained silent. Someone had to listen. Someone had to hear how it hurt and frightened you. And who better than the one who loved you most?

The first time I saw a man cry I was shocked. The second time I was relieved . . . relieved to know that he could feel as I did and seek comfort in the release of tears.

'Start counting . . . one . . . two . . . three . . . four, and just breathe quietly.'

How can anyone begin to imagine the terror of the patient counting himself into unconsciousness, knowing full well that when he wakes up, there may be a death sentence pinned to his report sheet?

Donald laughed and cracked jokes to cover the fear that consumed him. On the surface, he was calm and composed, but deep inside he was screaming with anguish and petrified by the thought of tomorrow.

The operation was at two p.m. I was told that it would take a couple of hours. I waited out that time in an agony of apprehension, while the mutilation of your body took place.

We had been told in advance what to expect. The growth was to be removed from the colon. At the same time any suspicious looking cells would be taken out, and a temporary by-pass (colostomy) created. This procedure would allow the newly joined segments to heal. As a result, all faeces would pass out through the wall of the abdomen, above the join, and be collected in a plastic bag attached to the skin. A biopsy would be performed to determine the extent of the involvement of surrounding lymph tissue. This was the key that would actually signal the final prognosis.

At four-thirty p.m. I could stand it no longer, and rang Phillip. He rang through and asked Donald's ward for the operation notes and read them to me over the phone: 'Large tumour obstructing the transverse colon and positive cells in surrounding lymph tissue.' I sat stunned and stared blankly out the window.

'Are you there, Ann?' I fought desperately with the scream that was rising in my throat. 'Ann, are you there?'

'Yes, Phillip, I'm here. I'm coming in right away.'

As I hung up, I became aware of the heavy silence in the room around me. With my head on my desk, I sobbed, great rasping, cruel sobs, that threatened to choke me.

'My God, he's going to die. Do you hear me? He's going to die.'

My whole life was taken away from me in those few moments. Everything that had ever seemed worthwhile or desirable, had gone. All that was left was this enormous, shrieking, throbbing pain. I think that was my moment of greatest loss. My understanding and realization were complete.

When I walked into the hospital room, my sense of loss was reinforced by your appearance. My love, you looked so ill – deathly white, deeply comatose and with lines of intense suffering in your face. In my anguish, all I could do was lean over you and whisper 'Oh, my darling', and tiptoe out again.

Georgette and Howard, close friends of ours, drove me home where Graeme was waiting for us. I stumbled towards him, groping for words in which to tell him, but he pushed aside my hand, bracing himself against the shock of his own pain. He was sixteen and a boy, and boys don't cry.

He and Howard went off to buy food, leaving Georgie and me sitting on the edge of the bed sipping neat brandy and weeping helplessly. Not many people would have dared to do as Georgie did, descend into my own private hell and share with me my most awesome sorrow. I could have endured it alone, but somehow her presence transformed the anguish into a strangely beautiful experience.

I'm still not sure what was born that night. Perhaps we witnessed the emergence of faith in the ability of the human mind to triumph over the frailty of the body. All I know is that her sharing of my pain, with love, understanding, and courage, helped me to survive that terrible night in March.

The warning signs had all been there: blood in the toilet;

pains in the tummy; age forty-plus; and a family history of cancer. In its early stages, Donald's tumour could easily have been removed. But it had already spread before the correct diagnosis was made.

• *April* •

We grieved separately and together, as we absorbed the full impact of the blow that had been dealt to us. At first, it was so big that we couldn't understand . . . we just simply couldn't comprehend the enormity of our tragedy.

You were normally a very funny man. Your sense of humour was probably your most remarkable quality. But quite suddenly we couldn't find the laughs. Tiring of tears and sadness, we searched diligently for other emotions. All we found were more tears and even greater sadness.

Easter passed us by. We were isolated by the shadow of your illness. You remained wrapped in a grey blanket of pain and misery, while I stood by, feeling helpless and futile.

From your bed, you could see a magnificent panorama of the lake, outlined by pure gold autumn leaves, and the deep blue hills behind. You told me that you found it difficult to relate to the scene below. Your pain and anxiety effectively cut you off from the outside world. It was like looking at a scene painted on the wall. It was hard to believe that there were people out there who could touch those trees and run the leaves through their fingers and feel the fresh breeze on their faces. The centre of our world was a hospital bed. Time is so elongated when you are in pain.

Sue, who was expecting her first baby, used to go over to the hospital on her way home from work. The two, who had always found pleasure in matching their wits with one another, talked endlessly about the things that concerned and interested them both.

The father looked with love and pride on his first-born who had already made her way into the adult world. And the child talked urgently and with concern, as she willed him to maintain his precarious hold on life. He used to watch her walk from the hospital, and wish her Godspeed with the new life growing within.

• *26 April* •

'You're just going to let him die, aren't you? He isn't ever going to come out of this stinking hovel, is he? He'll never come home to me now. And I *need* him, I need him.'

'Sit down, Ann, and tell me quietly and calmly what has gone wrong,' Phillip said steadily from the safety of the other side of his desk.

'He's getting weaker and weaker and he can't cope with this awful disease. I need him to come home again. Can't you see that? He must come home just one more time. We must be alone together in our own home. Can't you see that, you stupid man?'

Complications had arisen in the post-operative period that prevented him from going home as soon as we expected. The delay was beginning to depress Donald, and I was exhausted and overwrought. It just seemed to me that anyone who was as sick as Donald was, would never be able to go home.

But I was wrong. He did live to come home. And dear, kindly, compassionate Phillip recognized my anguish and spent many patient hours, sitting on the end of Donald's bed, explaining what he was doing and why. He took time to talk to both of us when we were together, so that we could build up a composite picture of hope and survival (even though temporary) to sustain us through this difficult convalescence.

He took great care to ensure that we thoroughly understood the medical situation at every stage of Donald's illness. We knew the disease had spread beyond the original tumour. We knew he could survive, but that he was unlikely to live more than five years. We had our hearts pinned on at least five years.

One evening, I was sitting beside Donald's bed quietly talking about the family and things I had been doing at work. Suddenly, he went deathly white and clutched his side.

'Call the sister, quickly. I'm bleeding.' All hell broke out and being the coward I am, I retreated to the far end of the corridor. I stood at the window and looked out into the friendly dark and wondered if I would ever be strong enough to help him. Tears splashed down my face as I leant my cheek wearily against the cold glass, trying to find strength.

A voice beside me said, 'Are you all right, Mrs MacDonald?' and a little nurse slipped her arms around my waist and gave me a warm hug. 'It will be all right,' she whispered. She couldn't have been more than nineteen. So where did she learn to empathize so strongly with a woman twice her age? Who told her that her patient's peace of mind was inextricably bound up in the welfare of those he loved?

Time and time again that dedicated little band of nurses went beyond the bounds of duty in their efforts to determine the best possible way to treat their bewildered and often frustrated patient and his family.

• *3 May* •

The saddest birthday of my life. You in hospital and in great pain. And yet, you found the strength to write me a beautiful letter telling me why you were so happy to be married to me and to be father to our children. Oh, my sweet!

It seemed so strange to have my birthday without you. The children seem very conscious of your absence. When I went to bed there was a tiny pottery bird on my bedside table, with no card.

• *May* •

Even while contemplating an imminent and early death, nostalgia for a life that has passed and been lived with joy and laughter forces great tears of despair from behind your closed eyes. Many times, you have seen death – the death of elderly friends and relatives whose time had come. No matter, they had lived full and useful, or dull and boring lives. Their demise was in line with past experience and present expectation. There was no threat to wife and children and friends. Only the elderly die.

But now the scene has changed. You are being asked to do the impossible, the unbelievable: look at your own death, try it on for size, see how it feels.

'Oh no, you're so wrong. I'm one of the thirty per cent who survive! You'll see, I'm strong. Unlike these others, I have so much to live for. I will survive. Come, little spouse, don't weep. You have nothing to weep for. We are going to dance on down the years together. God doesn't destroy love like ours. It's too rare and too precious.'

Maren had almost finished her degree when it fell to me to explain that her father was dying.

She came home for the vacation. It was a clear sunny day in May when I picked her up from the airport. We went down by the lake and walked to the carillon while I explained what was happening. I can't remember what I said. How do you tell a child that her father's life will soon be over? How do you explain that their friendship is drawing to a close?

Then the brutal shock of seeing him emaciated, ill and suffering. She handled it well. Chatted brightly about her courses and life on campus. In fact, I was beginning to wonder whether she had understood what I had said.

When it was time to leave, she kissed him brightly, said 'I'll be back soon' and gave a big cheerful grin as she closed the door.

Two paces down the corridor she fainted dead away.

Phillip had allowed Donald to come home for the weekend.

'Hey, gutless, come here. You're going to have to steel yourself and help me with this dressing. I just don't seem to be able to manage it on my own.'

I shuddered and his laughing eyes mocked me as he waited for my protest. Although my mother was a nurse, I have always had a quite exceptional aversion to wounds of any description. I just can't stand the sight of torn flesh. It's so unnatural. Fortunately, our children and animals have always been healthy and I had never even had to cope with a tonsillectomy.

'Have you tried lying flat on your back to change it?'

'Yes, but I haven't got three hands. You always said you loved me,' he taunted.

'I'll have to sit down and think about it. You didn't tell me this might happen. You know I can't even take the dog to the vet.'

I went out into the sun and sat by the pool for a bit. Everything looked so orderly and normal out there.

'Hurry up. I shall probably bleed to death before you make up your mind.'

Reluctantly, I got up and went back into the bedroom.

'All right. So just you remember how much I love you, to do this.'

'I will, my darling, I will.'

The ugly crimson incision scorched my brain, as I lifted off the dressing and saw for the first time what they had done to him.

• *End of June* •

The big day had come at last. He was coming home. Never mind that his suit hung in big loose folds. Never mind that he looked as weak as a kitten. Never mind that I was terrified something might go wrong. He was coming home.

As we walked into the house, we looked at one another and grinned with pure delight. It had happened, even as Phillip had said it would.

I made a cup of tea, glowing with pleasure. What it meant to us to share a cup of tea and our private thoughts in the quiet of our own home.

This was where we both belonged.

• *July* •

Donald desperately wanted to go back to work. We considered the possibility of going overseas, but his doctors advised that it would probably be a disaster. On learning this, Donald put the idea right out of his mind and concentrated on getting back to work.

To those of us who were obliged to front up to work every day, this didn't seem a very exciting prospect. But to Donald it represented a return to the world of normal people. It was the most positive way he could say 'I'm not sick.' It reassured him to don his suit and tie each day and simply go to work.

Unfairly perhaps, I was shocked by the welfare officer

who suggested that it might be rather traumatic for his colleagues to work with a man whose life-span was known to be limited. Rightly or wrongly, I felt they were privileged to see his courage and indomitable good humour at such close quarters.

• *August* •

Little did we realize how quickly time was running out on us. We had no idea that in a mere fragile three months, it would all be over. We were still walking around, going to work, and just being ourselves.

In fact, the last time you saw the surgeon he said, 'I don't need to see you again.' You came out with your newly restored life clutched firmly to your heart. We walked around the city in the sunshine, holding hands like children at a picnic.

We were so happy, so deliriously happy to be together with all that beastly illness behind us. The hateful restrictions of hospital life, the smells, the fear and the pain were gone. How incredibly wise we were to live in that bright, shiny new present, to savour the warmth and the pleasure of every moment. We enjoyed them and we loved it, and oh God, how I treasure the memory of it. I can only be thankful that we had the wisdom to use our time well. We loved, we laughed, and we played. We closed our minds to the past and we didn't think about the future. We had learnt our lesson, and learnt it well. The one thing in this life that you can be certain of is the present moment.

• *14 August* •

We went to the film of *The Magic Flute*. It was a stunning performance and one that we both enjoyed enormously. I wondered whether the trials of Pamina and Tamino were in some way similar to our own. The young lovers are told that to be worthy of being blessed by true love, they must endure a number of severe trials. Sarastro, the high priest, promises to aid and support them in their difficulties, and finally raises them to a state of perfect love.

We drove home with the music still washing quietly over our minds. It was like a gentle benediction on our love.

• 21 *August* •

Last night I went to bed early leaving Donald reading in his favourite chair and listening to music. I didn't hear him come to bed. He was very quiet.

This morning, I found a book still open by his chair. He had marked a poem by Christina Rossetti.

> Remember me when I am gone away,
> Gone far away into the silent land;
> When you can no more hold me by the hand,
> Nor I half turn to go, yet turning stay.
> Remember me when no more day by day
> You tell me of our future that you plann'd:
> Only remember me; you understand
> It will be late to counsel then or pray.
> Yet if you should forget me for a while
> And afterwards remember, do not grieve:
> For if the darkness and corruption leave
> A vestige of the thoughts that once I had,
> Better by far you should forget and smile
> Than that you should remember and be sad.

Oh, my love, my soul weeps for you.

• 22 *August* •

One Sunday morning you emerged from the bathroom swathed in a deep brown towel. (I shall remember that colour for the rest of my life.) Standing in front of the mirror you thoughtfully examined a swelling on one side of your chest. As I watched I saw the shadow of death pass over your face, and I began the long, slow, painful process of preparing myself for your eventual departure and my ultimate aloneness.

I agreed that you did look a little lopsided. We decided to visit the surgeon first thing in the morning.

The heaviness in my heart was indescribable. It had happened much sooner than we expected. Later in the morning an old Scottish friend of ours dropped in for a yarn. I marvelled at the way you talked as though nothing were amiss. Then you were called to the fence by a neighbour.

I flung myself at Alec and sobbed, 'Oh Alec, it's come back. The tumour has spread.' His beautiful voice thick with emotion, he held me close and whispered, 'Hang on, lass, hang on. And for God's sake keep smiling.' And I did keep smiling, though it nearly killed me. I suppose there is some merit in smiling when your heart is secretly breaking inside you.

• *23 August* •

The next day, X-rays were taken which showed a fresh tumour between the fifth and sixth ribs. This was inoperable and the only possible palliative lay in extensive radiotherapy, possibly combined with chemotherapy. Arrangements were made for admission to a large Sydney hospital the following day. The night before we left, Phillip rang up to see how things were going and to let us know he was thinking of us.

We were not shocked, so much as saddened beyond belief, to have the spread of the tumour confirmed. We had been well prepared by Donald's doctors. We knew the course the disease was likely to run, and we recognised the significance of the markers. We both understood what the surgeon was saying when he explained that he could do nothing more. Nevertheless, we had an extraordinary sense of having been abandoned.

However, Donald was not one to give up the struggle easily. And if radiotherapy and/or chemotherapy were going to give him even a few more months of life, he wanted to have it.

IV
In Search of the Healer

• *27 August 1976* •
Sydney

We left for Sydney on a beautiful, warm, spring morning. Emma, one of my colleagues and a very good photographer, came to take photos of the whole family before we left. Nothing was said. She was swift, imaginative, and efficient, and in her own super-sensitive way, empathized completely with the bravely smiling family. But the camera didn't lie. The suffering shown in those photos was immense.

We had always loved Sydney and were entranced as we drove into the city in the late afternoon sun. The room of our hotel overlooked Elizabeth Bay, with a magnificent view across the harbour. It was absolutely delightful being there on our own together. I really couldn't remember anything quite like it.

• *28 August* •

But next morning, we drearily accepted the bleak necessity for admission to a large ward, in a large and crowded hospital.

It took a week before the necessary ray treatment had been organized, an anxious, frustrating time. During the week, a full body scan was carried out. This revealed a whole patchwork of tiny new growths. The disease was now widespread and out of control. However, it was Donald's wish that treatment should proceed.

I went with him to his first session. An orderly arrived

with a wheelchair and was told brusquely by Donald that he would walk, thank you. 'Ha, that's all right. We'll be taking you on a stretcher before you're through, mate!', was the reply.

It was a long tortuous descent into the depths of the hospital. The waiting room was bleak and windowless, peopled with patients in varying stages of misery. It was not a reassuring sight. Many looked as though they would die before the massive machine could compete its task.

As we waited, I found my mind groping back to a similar scene described in Biblical times. But there was a difference. The Healer then was young, sympathetic, and spreading a message that men wanted to hear. Here, the patients were isolated by their tumours, screened off from the world around them by the disease that was growing even as they waited. And the healer – if indeed, you could describe this monstrous machine as a healer – was a cold, distant thing swinging aloft, controlled from outside the room by experts who watched the patient from behind protective glass. This healer produced endless weakness, nausea and other discomforts – and it might not heal. Perhaps it would only slow down the growth-rate of the malignancy. At worst, it did nothing.

• *September* •

Donald was transferred to a convalescent hospital in one of Sydney's suburbs for the last five weeks of his radiotherapy. As he was receiving only two minutes of treatment every twenty-four hours, it was not considered necessary to maintain a normal hospital bed for him.

The radiotherapy unit was closed at weekends, so he did not have to stay in this new hospital (known as the Annexe) on Saturday and Sunday.

As Graeme was sitting for his HSC, I remained in Canberra during the week. The usual arrangement was that I would fly down from Canberra on Friday and meet Donald at a hotel after his morning treatment. On Sunday I would catch a taxi to the airport, dropping him at the Annexe on the way.

The first time I did this, I felt guilty and depressed, as if I were leaving him alone to get on with his dying. Characteristically, Donald understood this. He kissed me with more than usual tenderness as he helped me into the car, then squeezed my hand and said, 'Don't worry, I'm all right.'

As we drove off, the taxi driver said cheerfully, 'Hubby sick, is he? What's wrong with him?'

'He has cancer,' I replied absentmindedly.

'Oh, Christ,' he exclaimed, and lapsed into gloomy, but eloquent silence.

My friend, Mary, had been awarded a scholarship by the French government, to live and work in Paris for six months. Her husband, Bob, was to remain in Canberra and join her for the last few weeks.

I was in Sydney with Donald when she left, and she rang from Mascot to say goodbye. Slowly it dawned on me that she was saying goodbye to Donald forever. It was most unlikely that his greatly weakened body would survive for another six months.

As I put down the phone I realized that my thought was shared. Donald said sadly, 'Give Mary a big hug when she comes back and tell her it has been a lot of fun knowing her.'

One lovely spring morning another friend, Anne, took me to Parsley Bay. We took off our shoes and went down to the little beach where I had so often played as a child. I have a vivid memory of laughing, teasing aunts and uncles and carefree, childish days full of warm sun and sand.

I went with Anne to try to recapture some of that sense of safeness – the 'God is in his heaven' kind of feeling. Stretched out on the sand, we ate our lunch and watched the sun sparkling on the water.

Suddenly, it all became too much for me. I found myself sobbing, 'Oh Anne, what am I going to do?'

'You will do as you have always done,' she said quietly. 'You will just keep on going, because you know that's what you have to do. Donald himself will help you and we will all be giving a big push from behind. Don't worry. I know you'll do it well.'

She told me about her visits to Donald during the week, when I was back in Canberra.

'He never talks about illness or the hospital. His mind is as active and lively as ever. He wants to know all about your father and what you were like before he met you. We talk of books and plays and operas. And all the time, he's so brave. So you must be brave too.'

As the shadows lengthened, I left Parsley Bay, feeling stronger and calmer and a teeny bit braver.

During his first three weeks in the Annexe, Donald imposed a rigid discipline on himself, a programme of activity that kept him out of the ward as much as possible. He was up and dressed by eight a.m., and after the daily trip to the hospital he would walk and explore the surrounding district. He read, wrote in the sun, and spent many hours talking to his fellow inmates, who found him a jovial and entertaining companion.

But by mid-September he was crippled by radiation sickness. Nursing staff were not in constant attendance, and he would have to decide between lying in bed, acutely nauseated and in great pain, or getting up and looking for a member of staff to request medication.

Individual patient dosage was determined by a brief visit each morning from a young resident at the hospital, who prescribed the medication for the following twenty-four hours. Donald's and my repeated requests for stronger pain relief fell on deaf ears. Six weeks before his death, the dosage of two digesics every six hours remained unchanged, despite extensive bony metastasis, a spreading of the cancer throughout the body.

> The grief that does not speak
> Whispers the o'er-fraught heart, and bids it break.

When I arrived at the hotel, I found you already in the bedroom waiting. Without a word, you took me in your arms and held me close and your whole body shook with uncontrollable sobs. You were no longer able to hide from me the immensity of your anguish. Your grief was violent, tempestuous, and destructive and I felt totally surrounded by your sorrow and despair. You had finally acknowledged that for you, there were no more tomorrows.

'It's a little breath of old Lindfield,' Anne explained as she handed me a fragrant posy of spring flowers from her garden. All weekend, we were gladdened by the delicate blooms and grateful for their presence in the sterile room and alien atmosphere of the inner city.

• 29 *September* •

Final ray treatment today. We waited in the freezing, underground waiting room, for hours. The pain was obviously very bad. Twice I had to ask the sister in charge for digesics and a glass of water.

We came to Sydney because radiotherapy wasn't yet available in Canberra. But was there any point? What's the use of more life if the quality is so awful? Were we doing anything more than wasting precious time away from home and family?

When should you stop treatment and simply try to appreciate what is left of your life? The radiotherapy makes him too sick to enjoy anything. There must be a better way. Perhaps we should have stayed home and just waited – together.

If I were a painter, I would paint a picture to depict how I felt at that moment. It would show my skull splitting clean down the middle, and my brain bursting out coloured deep blue, purple, and magenta, from being severely compressed for so long.

The specialist had arranged to see us at ten a.m. Our plane was leaving at midday and he wanted to give last minute instructions. Donald, pale, thin, nauseated and trembling, was having difficulty sitting up in the chair in the small draughty corridor. We waited and waited and waited.

At last he was free. 'Well now, let's see. We have given you the maximum allowable dosage of radiation and the tumour in your chest is slightly smaller. When you get home, your doctor will arrange for appropriate cytotoxic treatment and you will take it from there. Have you any questions?'

Donald shifted uneasily, and said, 'Yes, what exactly is the state of play at this time? In other words, at what stage in my life or my death, am I now?'

The phone on the desk shattered the silence.

'Oh, hi there, Graham, how are you? Yes I'm fine, just back from a couple of weeks on Heron Island so I ought to be. Yes, actually she's leaving for Europe in ten days time and is very busy making last minute arrangements . . .'

The conversation lasted fourteen minutes by the clock, until a mutually convenient date for a dinner party was established. But it wasn't fourteen minutes – it was fourteen hours that ticked away, while one desperately ill man waited to hear the verdict.

'Now then, where were we? Oh yes, well, it will be up to your physician to work out a therapeutic regime that will keep you at work as long as possible. And after that . . .' He shrugged.

We caught the plane home and drove straight to the hospital, where Phillip took in the situation at a glance. He prescribed large quantities of Pethidine for Donald.

I gave him his pills at four p.m. and had the satisfaction of seeing the first smile on his face in weeks, as he settled back into his very own bed that looked out on to a tiny secluded courtyard.

V
About Dying

• *September 1976* •
Canberra

As a family, we have always been very conscious of the need to have a place of refuge and peace within our own home. To this end we built a courtyard surrounded by a high brick wall, on to which the drawing room and our bedroom opened. The drawing room, with its muted colours and walls lined with our favourite books is a very restful room.

We didn't really plan the courtyard. It just grew. Donald and I used to sit out on the bare, brown earth and dream of stately fountains, waterfalls, orchids, the lot. It was great fun. Piece by piece, we placed the paving slabs and arranged the garden around them.

Then I had an unfortunate lapse from commonsense. I dreamed of a large fishpond, wandering like a miniature Lake Burley Griffin through the courtyard. This nearly cost me my marriage. It was okay when we started, but halfway through, Donald suddenly realized what a damned fool, impractical idea it was. At this stage, we had a large gaping, muddy hole in the ground and no idea what to do next. For three weeks Donald went to golf and refused to join me in my dreams.

Winter was coming on and it was pretty obvious to every visitor that the man of the house had failed dramatically in what was clearly a relatively simple project. So he lined it with concrete. I got into terrible trouble because I filled it with water and leaned little plants over the edge before the concrete was properly 'cured'.

Slowly, however, the pond became the focal point of the entire courtyard. And now, it is full of waterlilies and fish fat enough to fry. Around the edge grow wild blue irises and catmint, while honeysuckle and ivy tumble down the wall. In the corner there is a crabapple tree that every autumn produces enough rosy little apples to turn into two or three jars of clear red jelly.

As his days drew to a close, Donald sought the comfort of the courtyard, sitting quietly reading or watching the fish. I planted a pale apricot rose beside his chair.

His view narrowed as he was forced back to bed, but still the garden helped him to maintain his hold on life as he watched his time shrink and his world grow dim.

And I? I didn't have time to look at the garden. My time was yet to come. Oh yes, the day came all right, when I had all the time in the world to sit in the courtyard and think about my life, or lack of it.

• 2 *October* •

I had to call Phillip tonight. He came to the house because Donald was in so much pain. He talked quietly and reassuringly to Donald. As he walked back through the house, he looked at me with an anxious frown and said, 'I'm sorry Ann; he hasn't got long to live.'

'I can't believe it. I just *can't* believe it! In another three or four weeks, it will all be over.'

'He has a lesion pressing on his brain.'

'Oh God, where will we find the strength?'

• *4 October* •

His condition deteriorated rapidly. Even so, neither of us realized how close we were to the end. When Phillip suggested that it would be necessary for him to re-enter hospital for a day or two, I took him along quite trustingly. It was only later that I realized I had taken him away from his home for the last time. Indeed, it was I who unwittingly betrayed him. He never came back.

• *7 October* •

It rains and it rains and it rains. And I am tired . . . so tired. All I can do is draw the next breath . . . and the next . . . and the next. I have to keep going.

Donald too is very tired and will be thankful when it's all over. Mercifully, the painkillers are controlling the pain very well.

I really think that given the wherewithal and the opportunity, I could administer the fatal needle that would ensure a speedy and dignified death. I don't dispute the right of the doctor to make this decision on moral, ethical, or religious grounds. I am merely defending the right of the individual to decide that a terminal illness should be ended while the patient is still capable of appreciating a quiet finish to an increasingly intolerable existence. Interestingly enough, I have never yet spoken to a doctor who would not wish this for himself or close members of his family. So is the cowardice theirs or mine?

Terminal cancer seems to follow a predictable and measurable course in its final stages. It should be possible to choose a point at which the patient may, at his or her own request, be given a lethal dose, without involving the doctor in culpable manslaughter. This seems a logical therapeutic stage in the care of the terminally ill.

The children are stunned by their father's illness. He has always seemed to them an enormously reliable and competent man, who towers over the rest of us in stature and personality.

So how can he be mortally ill? It simply can't happen. Just put him to bed and feed him on ginger ale and vegemite sandwiches and he'll be right.

When Mum said this wasn't true; that in fact he was dying, they thought, she's wrong. She has to be wrong. Mum can't even tell a joke without getting the punch line wrong.

Sue searched diligently for signs of improvement. Maren, mistrusting my judgement, checked with Phillip and was devastated when the prognosis was confirmed. Graeme turned his back and refused to believe me, but now the evidence of his own eyes was forcing him to accept what was happening.

'You'll need a holiday when this is over. Don't go too far away; You're too tired. Just go far enough for it to be different. Why don't you try Vila? Brush up your French. Do you good.'

'Shall I go by myself?'

'Yes, I think you'll want to sleep a lot and you'll need time to lick your wounds in private. I don't think you should inflict your mood on someone else's holiday. And later on, when you feel stronger, you must go for a long, lazy stay in the Greek Islands.'

'Will you be there?'

'Of course, I will. My spirit will watch over you tenderly, and laugh to see you so happy.'

I would give anything to be able to take his place for a while. If only we could take shifts, so that he could have every alternate period free from the whole ghastly nightmare. It hardly seems fair that the same soul should be battered and broken all the time.

Even so, there were great pools of happiness that sometimes found their way into your sickroom. There was the bright, sunny morning in October when Sue and Alan proudly brought their new baby to meet his grandfather. You were too weak to nurse him and were content to watch me rock him in my arms, sharing the tenderness I felt for the tiny new life who had found his way into our family – and who would grow up without any memory of the dying man who smiled at him with such love.

The day is young and the birds begin to stir. Pale grey light is creeping through the vines by the window. I nearly always witness the birth of the new day now; it's all too easy to lose the threads of sleep. I find it a surprisingly soothing time of day.

Often I write a long letter to Donald, telling him about things I find difficult to express in words. And he, in his lonely hospital bed a few miles away, writes me some of the most tender letters I have ever read.

This strange little correspondence brings a stability to our relationship that might not exist otherwise. When we're together, it's so hard to get beyond the pain . . . my pain and his pain. Two pains. Two quite separate pains . . . with a different origin and a different end.

But when we write, we leave the pain alone. We talk about other things: deeper, more permanent things.

We discuss our plans for the future. Donald has spent a

lot of time visualizing my first twelve months of widowhood. He has tried to anticipate the problems I may encounter and has discussed them with me at length. He feels that I should keep my present job for a year. He has also advised me not to sell the house or the car during those first twelve months. He sees this as a time when it will be difficult to make rational decisions. He has talked to me about all three children and told me how he believes each one will develop. He is confident that as a family we will draw even closer together after his death.

'You still wear your pearls?'

'Yes. Why not? You know how I love them.'

'I just thought . . . they say pearls are unlucky.'

'Well, we knew that when I wanted to wear them on my wedding day, but we weren't scared, were we?'

'No, of course not. May I hold them?'

He passed the creamy pearls through his fingers and sighed. 'All I wanted in the world was to make you happy. And now I'm bringing you more sorrow than any human being should ever have to bear. Maybe pearls really are for tears.'

Truly, each pearl still glistens like a big frozen tear – but such very beautiful tears. I wouldn't be without them for worlds.

Sometimes I marvel at the way I went on buying you clothes right up to the very end. Fiercely denying that a time would ever come when you would no longer need those clothes. Even as they split the sleeve of your pyjama jacket, to make way for the battery of drips that connected you to this life, I smilingly assured you that I would soon sew it up again.

And you treacherously agreed, knowing full well that I never mend anything. Oh darling, what else could we do?

What good would it have done anyone if we had screamed and raged and demanded that everyone should witness our grief and acknowledge our loss, before it was upon us. We all knew, those of us who surrounded your bed, day after day. I still remember the faces and the gentle eyes of the nurses dressed in pink or blue as they watched our approaching agony.

• *16 October* •

The Natural History of the Spaghettis was finally finished today. The saga of the Spaghetti family who lived high in the Italian Alps in a little wooden hut has been woven in and around our family life ever since you said to Graeme many years ago: 'Didn't you know that spaghettis wear handknitted cardigans and yellow gumboots? Goodness me, doesn't your mother ever tell you anything? How very ignorant you are.'

The Spaghetti family resembled the MacDonald family in many ways. The Spaghettis had three very similar, noisy, irrational, loveable children, who cut holes in their bedspread and lost pages of daddy's thesis in much the same way that our children did. The younger Spaghettis' baby brother drilled holes in the drawing room floor with the same implacable calm as the MacDonalds'. But by and large, their parents were inclined to laugh about it. And sometimes, the Spaghettis had adventures we could never afford to have, like holidays in the Swiss Alps!

Later, as the children grew up, they begged you to write the stories out before you forgot them. You laughingly agreed that when you had more time you would publish them for the benefit of other culturally deprived families.

But it was the advent of your own grandson and the imminence of your death that finally prompted you to commit it to paper and dedicate it to 'Edward and all those who follow after him.'

• *20 October* •

Phillip had to go to Melbourne for a week. He knew how heavily we had come to rely on him, both as a physician and a friend. It disturbed him to think that Donald might die during his absence and that I would be left without his support at the time I would need it most. He discussed the problem with us both. Such was the quality of the relationship built up during the previous months.

I hold in the highest possible esteem the man who took on this difficult and demanding role. Without him Donald and I would have been lost. As it was, his friendship enabled us to see ourselves as a part of a trio, setting off on a journey together. Phillip was at the helm, Donald was a helpless and unwilling passenger, and I – well I felt as though I did all the rowing.

Because he was so concerned about leaving us alone, Phillip suggested calling in a psychiatrist to help us. This seemed sensible and desirable, so we agreed.

Well, it was a disaster. I don't know why it was a disaster, but it was. I suspect that the fault was my own. I may have been too hasty in rejecting his help or I may have been too frightened to follow his lead. My main feeling was of overwhelming and terrifying threat. I was finding it difficult enough to cope with the day-to-day demands on my strength, without confronting my widowhood in advance. I found questions such as, 'Do you think you will go mad?' inappropriate and devastating. The short answer was, 'Yes, any minute now!'

After a couple of these sessions, I declined further 'help' and decided to carry on alone.

• *21 October* •

I was very conscious of Phillip's absence from the hospital. I felt insecure and unstable and so did Donald. We missed his warmth and honesty. The residents who had taken his place were young and unresponsive, and unable or unwilling to comprehend our approaching disaster.

You stupid, incompetent, unheeding boy. Why do you sit at your desk and scribble endlessly? Look into my eyes, damn you, and tell me what is happening in this godawful institution. Don't avoid me. You are part of this, whether you want to be or not. Don't just sit there pretending you can't hear my cries of anguish. Oh God, you never will hear . . . and you are going to be a doctor for the rest of your days.

Perhaps they didn't understand that I was not accusing them of allowing him to die. I was not asking them to intervene. I was only asking them to share with us . . . to share as Phillip had done.

It's no use arguing that this isn't part of the function of a physician. Because when all else has failed, this is the greatest and most wonderful gift a doctor has to offer. And may God give all of them the strength and compassion they need to go on offering it for the whole of their professional lives.

• *April–December* •

One very beautiful and continuing thread ran through Donald's illness, encompassed his death, and carried on into my life beyond.

To put this in context, I must explain that the nature of my work brings me into contact with a small group of very able doctors. One of these is Michael, who when he was young had to choose between continuing his studies in medicine or English language and literature. Finally, he settled on medicine, arguing that he could still pursue his interest in literature as a hobby.

It was a strange set of circumstances that prompted Michael to give up his lunch hour every week, to read Tolkien's *Lord of the Rings* to Margaret and myself. We are both children at heart, and still love nothing better than to curl up in an armchair and listen to a born story-teller.

The tale of the search for the ring transported us into other worlds and other times, where our imaginations roamed freely and filled our minds with magic. It helped to soothe the harsh reality that had become my day-to-day existence. For that brief space in time, my mind centred on the adventures of Frodo and Pippin and Sam (I always identified with Sam). I was free to ponder the complexity of the role of the great Gandalf. And so the time passed, and Michael offered me a beautiful and sensitive release from the torture of reality.

It was some weeks after Donald died that we finished 'The Return of the King,' and Frodo took ship and sailed out into the High Sea 'until he beheld white shores and beyond them a fair green country under a swift sunrise. But to Sam the evening deepened to darkness as he stood at the Haven; and as he looked at the grey sea he saw only a shadow on the waters that was soon lost in the West. There still he stood far into the night, hearing only the sigh and murmur of the waves on the shores of Middle-earth, and the sound of them sank deep into his heart.'

• *October* •

What a mercy it is that animals cannot speak. Had it been possible for our well-loved family labrador to tell us what she was feeling, we would have been utterly destroyed. Always deeply affected by departures and goodbyes, she viewed our holidays with the utmost gloom. The very sight of the suitcases being brought down from the attic threw her into the depths of depression for days on end.

The return home of any member of the family was always an occasion for great rejoicing. The children often remarked how a bad day at school could be completely obliterated by Georgie's warm welcome home. She always seemed to know when someone was missing and would take up her place by the door, head on paws and eyes fixed on the end of the drive, waiting for the latecomer.

How did she know you were ill, or worse still, dying? Did your lengthy absences in hospital alert her to the danger? She seemed to grieve for your absence, even while we still had hope.

I did remember to thank the sister who smuggled her into the hospital a few weeks before you died. Frustrated and unable to reach you, she sat and devoured you with her huge brown eyes. That was the last time she saw you.

With characteristic good sense, she soon accepted me as leader of the pack and now obeys me with the same alacrity and unquestioning loyalty she showed you. But still she gazes longingly up the drive ready to leap up with that special love which was always yours.

• 22 *October* •
To Mary in Paris

Dear Mary, Home, 4.30 a.m.

As you can see, I'm keeping my usual early morning vigil with the sparrows. I don't really mind so much now. Having accepted this as a fact of life, I have managed to convince myself that it's incredibly luxurious to lie in bed at this hour, with a cup of tea and thin bread and butter, listening to Bizet's *Pearlfishers* (which can always draw a sob out of me), and writing a letter or reading a book.

I met Geoff R. in the lift yesterday and he said in that tight, gritty voice of his, 'Have you got the report on the data bases written up yet?' I found myself looking at him in wonderment and thinking, 'Geoff, do you know what it feels like to watch the other half of your soul die by inches?' If he really wants to know, I'm not doing anything. If anyone so much as mentions data bases, I spring a leak. I flit nervously from one task to another and accomplish nothing.

The strange thing is that I can sit down and write several pages to you with great enjoyment, but having to do something in a precise understandable format is quite beyond me.

I know instinctively that this is the worst time. Donald dead and out of pain can't be as bad as Donald barely alive and suffering. Last night, I arrived when the sister was giving him a back rub. They said to go in, but Mary, I couldn't. I just can't bear to see his poor, pathetic, wasted body. Donald, who seven months ago, was so tall and fit and full of life. This pitiful skeleton with the wandering mind is all that's left to me. They embarked on further surgery last Thursday. I don't ask questions anymore and neither does Donald. What's the use? One can only presume they are doing the best they can.

One day, when he was not quite so sick, Donald said to me, 'You know, you are putting on the best performance of Pagliacci the world has ever seen.'

When it comes to boosting up my courage, a remark like that takes some beating.

Did I tell you that Donald celebrated his fiftieth birthday while we were in Sydney? Anne, a very old friend of mine, brought him a box of the most exquisite neenish tarts I have ever tasted. He was too sick to eat them, so I ate twenty-two neenish tarts in two days and didn't even feel sick . . .

Mary dear, the time has flown around to seven a.m. It's time for the ritual grapefruit. It's a beautiful day and I think perhaps God is in His heaven.

Lots of love,
Ann

Half a million odd socks! I don't know where they all come from. I always buy pairs. Somewhere in the world, there must be an equally inefficient housewife who has the other half. Perhaps we could arrange to meet someday and do a deal.

Donald is on fifteen-minute observation. The attention he gets is absolutely fantastic. One thing that interests me is the way the nurses draw closer to him, knowing that he is dying. His needs are anticipated with a tenderness and devotion that is almost spiritual in its intensity. Everything possible is done for his comfort.

I feel it is very difficult for him, in these last stages of decay, to be surrounded by those of us who are actually witnessing the ultimate humiliation of his disease. I try to hide my abhorrence and sit calmly beside his bed, apparently oblivious to the medical procedures going on around me.

'Promise me you will marry again if you want to.'

'Oh darling, be human. I can't.'

'No, you must promise. It's very important. Some day you may look back and wonder what I would have thought. And I want you to know you would be doing so with my deepest blessing.'

He leant back wearily on his pillow, and slow tears crept from behind his closed eyes.

I kept on working. Not because I needed the money or liked the job, but because I knew it would be a fragile link with reality after he was gone. It was a fiendish existence. Awake at four; at the hospital at eight; at work at nine; hospital for lunch; back to work; home for tea; back to the hospital; and then home to bed . . . probably not to sleep. Next day, same again.

Although Donald was dying, life went on in a maddening and irritatingly regular manner. Nothing stopped. Dishes had to be washed. Clothes still got dirty. The animals had to be fed. Bills had to be paid. The carpet needed to be vacuumed.

It was like a variation of the Mad Hatter's tea party. A little voice inside me was chanting 'Faster, Ann, faster. You'll have to do better than this. Faster.'

The sights, sounds and smells of the hospital are a constant reminder of the steady progress of your disease. Deep in your heart is the certain knowledge that only death will release you from the sight of these four walls. No amount of compassionate nursing can alter the fact that you will remain here until you die.

Loved ones pause from the daily round of activities to take up their vigil by your bedside. They keep a faithful watch. But some day they will come no more. Because it will all be over. You will have ceased to exist.

These are the thoughts that must pass behind your fixed and tortured gaze. These are the thoughts that prevent you from reading the daily newspapers or listening to the family gossip. They are no longer relevant. You just sit and endure and wait out your sentence.

'The Queen Has Flu' is the headline in this morning's paper. Poor darling, she probably feels dreadful!

I went to the hospital early and found Donald looking very ill. Suddenly, I felt completely bereft and collapsed sobbing in his arms. As he stroked my hair, he said gently, 'Yes, I know . . . you're so lonely. But you will be all right.'

• *November* •

Maren, you cried and cried when you were born. I still feel sad when I think of it. You had been forced out into the reality of your brand new life, leaving behind the warmth and shelter you had known for nine beautiful months. Suddenly, it was all gone and you were lonely.

You cried again tonight and I was powerless to help you. You were going back to university, knowing you would never see your father again, and you wanted to say goodbye. It was heartbreaking and yet strangely beautiful.

As I waited outside, I wondered what a dying man says to his daughter. I heard a cry like the cry of a wounded animal and you emerged quietly weeping.

> And you, my father, there on the sad height,
> Curse, bless, me now with your fierce tears, I pray.
> Do not go gentle into that good night.
> Rage, rage against the dying of the light.

• *2 November* •
9.30 p.m.

The hospital is dark and still, surrounding the silence in this one room.

'You must get very tired with the wax dripping down your hands.'

Startled into wakefulness, I asked him what he meant.

'You remind me of a mediaeval saint, sitting there keeping a silent vigil, with a lighted candle in your hands. You are keeping a vigil aren't you?'

'Yes, my darling, I am keeping a vigil and will go on keeping it for as long as it is necessary.'

I feel sure that everyone needs to know that someone will keep watch with them for the rest of their life. I'm sure this must be terribly important. Don't let anyone die lonely.

• *3 November* •

'Bob, I want him to die. Can you understand that? I just want it to be over.'

I searched his face anxiously for shock and condemnation. But there was none. Just compassion, overwhelming, heartbreaking compassion. Because he was a doctor, as well as my friend, I could tell him my guilty secret. For the rest of the world, I had to go on being the resolute little wife, bravely supporting her dying husband. But underneath it all, I was a hopeless coward, trying to stifle the ignoble thoughts that persisted in coming to the surface.

Why couldn't I say: 'My husband's dying of cancer, and I'm dying of grief . . . but I'm making more fuss than he is.'

The only child we had at home during Donald's illness was Graeme, our youngest. He was in his final year at high school and sitting matriculation at the end of the year. Sensing that he was under considerable strain as he witnessed the daily deterioration of his father, I rang the headmaster of his school. I explained that Donald was ill and dying and that I would be grateful if he would mention this to the staff concerned and perhaps the school could help me in offering a little moral support to a child who was about to sustain a massive loss.

It was only very much later that I learned that his response to my plea was to call up Graeme and deliver a 'Now listen son, you pull your socks up. Don't imagine you will get any special treatment just because your father's ill.'

When the death-notice appeared in the paper, staff and students alike were saddened and shocked to learn that young 'Ern' had been fighting such a difficult battle all alone. Graeme hadn't told anyone . . . and neither had the headmaster.

How can I tell you that I am slowly detaching myself from your physical being, and looking beyond to the life spark that is really you? How to explain that the crumpled heap of bones and transparent skin, all that remains of your physical self, no longer matters? It's the innate spark that is the real you and even I can see that this is something that will remain with me.

Nobody has thought to tell me about dying. I know a lot about birth, having given exciting birth to three lovely, healthy children. But death is still a mystery. No one has explained what happens, and I haven't had the wit to ask.

By the strangest coincidence, a letter arrived today from a very close friend in New Zealand, whose husband died of leukemia. It was an impassioned plea that I be with you when you die. She urged me to remain quiet and calm ('hospitals don't like noisy, hysterical relatives').

'Don't cry, little one. Keep calm. If I can do it, you can. But insist upon being there, both for your sake and Donald's. Talk to him quietly and tell him how much you love him and stay there until you are sure he has passed on. There's nothing to be afraid of.

'And stop crying when you go to see him. It must grieve him to see you so sad. Don't cry, don't think, don't do anything – just exist. Don't let that strength you have slip for one moment. Just keep going.'

It was the end-of-school social. Graeme didn't have anything to wear and shuffled moodily around the boys' wear department. It was a depressing scene. Nothing was right. I recognized the symptoms; I'd been there before.

Looking bored and unhappy, he went across to suits. 'Everyone else is wearing a suit' he moaned. I doubted this, but let it pass.

Eventually, he settled on a light wool suit that cost an arm and a leg. Naturally.

Later, when I was telling his father, I complained about the futility of spending so much on a still growing boy.

'Nonsense,' he said. 'It's terribly important. This may be your last chance to show him that it's nice to dress up sometimes. We don't want to condemn him to jeans and desert boots for the rest of his life.'

When the day came, Graeme agreed to go via the hospital on his way to the dance. Graeme is finding it very hard to cope with Donald's rapid deterioration. His once tall, capable father no longer has the strength that always impressed the small boy. The frail, dying man has no place in his memory.

As Graeme stood in the doorway looking so young and fresh and vulnerable, Donald's tired eyes lit up with pride and approval. It comforts him to see his youngest child moving with confidence into an adult world.

The steady ticking of the grandfather clock slows down my heartbeat. The old clock has been marking off the hours of my life for as long as I can remember. It was part of the peace and warmth of my parent's home and now it is built into the memory of my children.

At the moment, I have a tendency to lie awake at night and listen to its gentle chiming of the hours. How much more time will it measure off for you, my love? Will it stop when you are gone? Or will it be like my own poor faithless heart, that threatens to go on beating, long after yours has stopped.

• 4 *November* •

My hand traces the outline of your jaw. How else can I pour out the tenderness that rises to meet your despair? How else do I teach my fingers to remember the lines of your beloved face?

There is so little I can do for you now. Hands more skilled

than mine have taken over the job of caring for you. The desolation of this final deprivation is almost too much for me. I haven't quite got the strength to accept my own ineptitude in the face of your need.

• *5 November* •

My head aches, my back aches and my soul aches. There is no room for any other feeling. I don't even have the energy to register despair. I'm incapable of feeling anything other than overwhelming fatigue.

As Stewart Alsop observed, 'A dying person needs to die, as a sleepy person needs to sleep.'

I spend most of my time curled up in a chair beside Donald's bed. I need to be close to him. I want to hold his hand and massage his feet and show that no matter how bad it is, I care.

It's lonely for both of us now.

• *6 November* •

By a miracle I heard the phone ring just after midnight to say that he was sinking fast and I would have to hurry. As I drove, I prayed wildly that I would be in time and that I would know what to do.

When I arrived they thought I was too late, but I raced into the room, calling him by name. He stirred slowly, opened his eyes and said 'Hullo darling, what are you doing here so late?'

Even as he was dying, he remembered to say the things that would be most precious to me in the heartbreaking days to follow.

He was thirsty and I went to get iced water and thought it strange that I was doing such an ordinary thing.

We talked a bit and shared our thoughts. He lay back exhausted, his paper-white hands caressing the bedspread. I knew the conversation was almost over and would never be repeated.

Suddenly, he seemed to remember what was happening and whispered urgently 'I love you, darling. You'll never know how much you mean to me.' I looked into his eyes and saw his love stored up for me to take a last look and remember for all time.

And how was it for him? That I cannot say, for he died and no longer told me what he saw or felt. But all my heightened awareness assured me that this was how he wanted it. It seemed so right that I should hold him and comfort him as he died. The moment came when I knew that his empty eyes were staring at a future in which I had no part.

I said a prayer for the repose of his soul and walked from the room with the certain knowledge that I left nothing that was mine behind me.

VI
In the Silent Place of Grief

• *November 1976* •

From far away in New Zealand, Dorothy sent me flowers – pale gold roses and blue delphiniums that soothed my soul. After dinner (when I should have been washing up) I did what you would have expected me to do. I took my flowers to the church and arranged them in a large bowl.

Two young girls with fair hair hanging loose over their shoulders and a young man with a gentle smile were practising with a guitar. They were going to sing at a wedding the next Saturday.

It was infinitely peaceful listening to them and knowing they were happy. Even now, I cannot feel your death brings total sadness. The world still seems to hold remarkable beauty and quiet happiness. There are still people holding hands and smiling and falling in love.

I stood back to admire the flowers and felt that we had truly fulfilled our marriage contract, as you and I had understood it.

I cried myself to sleep last night, for the first time in weeks. Sheer fatigue seems to be my worst enemy. I dreamt of an urgent need to talk to Donald . . . only to find I didn't have his phone number . . . Oh darling.

I feel as though I am kneeling before the whole of mankind, hands outstretched, saying, 'I am empty. I have no more to offer, nothing further to give. Please help me. Don't just pity me and walk away. For God's sake, help me.'

The shadow of my other life has gone, leaving me shivering in a corner by myself. The floor around me is grey, all grey. All the colour has been drained out of my beautiful world, and it too is grey. The warm goodness has left me; left me throbbing with a pain so sharp that the pieces fracture and then merge together in one soul-shattering stab. Frozen by loneliness and with eyes clouded by the events of the immediate past, I huddle by myself, waiting for the years to pass.

And yet I lie. My friends are all there. The children are stretching out to me. But I cannot reach them. Their compassion goes unheeded, as my mind stares at the wall of silence in front of me.

• *10 November* •
To Mary in Paris

Dear Mary,

Thus begins day five without Donald. He's gone, Mary. It's all over. With the breaking of the dawn came my new life . . . a life I don't want and have to accept. Oh Mary, Mary, why did he go? My loss feels so enormous. I could die with the pain of it. I won't tell you about Donald's last few days. Bob can do that some time when you are feeling all warm and loved and secure.

The funeral service, in spite of being a funeral, was beautiful. The little stone church was aglow with light and fragrant with flowers. Everyone had remembered my love of flowers. Friends brought them fresh from their own gardens. A small posy of cornflowers and yellow daisies held my attention. Owen, the rector, read from the Bible we had used for our wedding. The births of our children are recorded in the back in Donald's firm handwriting, and now, strangely, the death of Donald is there in mine.

Sue and Alan brought their baby and halfway through the service I heard him snuffling behind me. It was an unbelievably comforting sound. My bond with the children suddenly seemed tangible and overwhelmingly important.

Friends and family had joined to share a common pain and a common loss. And yet, when we all returned to the house after the service, we talked and laughed as we would have done had he still been with us. The feeling of warmth and friendship seemed to expand and grow and surround us. We were all held by the spell of the person who had brought us there. It wasn't a time for weeping, but a time for laughing and remembering.

I'm thinking of taking a couple of weeks holiday fairly soon. I haven't the energy to go far or be very enterprising. I just want to lie in the sun, somewhere we have never been together.

Bob has been around a number of times since Donald died and has been incredibly patient, as he listens for the millionth time to my account of what happened and how bad I feel. My poor mind feels so dented and bruised and I do rant on so.

I have no regrets, Mary, just the deepest possible sadness that it's over. Those wonderful years have drawn to a close. This isn't much of a letter. I guess what I really wanted to say was that Bob helped me through some of the most painful and most precious hours of my life. Thank you, Mary.

Ann

The tears rise up and spill over, splashing endlessly into the empty space around me.

It has to be. It's useless to ask why. I am a human being

grieving . . . and I must be allowed to grieve my fill and do so in peace.

Mark used to enjoy playing with our children. He borrowed freely from our family life. In between eating mountains of spaghetti and discussing the political scene and the state of the world with Donald and me, he sat on the floor with the kids. Together, they built extensive rail systems and intricate highway networks, covered with tiny matchbox cars.

His real masterpiece, however, was the merry-go-round he built for them out of Meccano. It was a nasty wet day and they had been pestering him for something on a really grand scale. In vain, he protested that he was a school-teacher, not a civil engineer. Then slowly a plan formed in his mind and he began to assemble the pieces of red and green steel. It was truly brilliant. I have never loved a Meccano model so much and the children still remember Mark's merry-go-round.

That was twelve years ago. We haven't seen him since we left New Zealand and now he has a family of his own.

Just a little while ago, I opened a cable that linked our lives together again: 'Please accept my deepest sympathy. A great man has passed. Kua hinga totara nui o te au Maori me te au Pakeha haere e hou. Arahanui. Mark.'

Roughly translated, this means, 'The mighty totara has fallen, and the Maori and the Pakeha weep. Farewell my friend. Go to your rest.'

Oh Mark.

• 21 November •
From Elaine in New Zealand

Dearest Ann,

Your letter of sixteenth November came and I knew what it must say. I took it away, and read it alone, lying and crying on my bed. There's nothing to say now. All sorts of things have been going through my mind and I have composed many letters to you, but they all seem too much or too little, and there is nothing I can say to comfort you.

I only read your letter through once. I just feel too sad about it all to read it again yet. Somehow, I had left you and Donald away back twenty or so years ago, still young, happy and gay, with that big, bouncy baby. I never thought of you as leaving that life and now you have come so far. At least Donald saw his children grow up and held his grandson . . .

Stay put in your house. I feel if I move, I lose all that is left of Allan – things he's touched, windows he's looked out, chairs he's sat in.

It's a very strange time you are going through now. Like being in a glass box somehow, and seeing everything in slow motion. Looking down at your hand and thinking in a detached way, 'that's part of me'. Driving the car and thinking how strange that you are doing it. How strange that you aren't lying on the floor screaming. You are so completely helpless. I know how you feel. I do know.

Remember, no one can do this for you. It is entirely up to you. And you can get through this time – for Donald's sake and your children, of course you can. If I can, you can.

Lovingly,
Elaine

There is a gap in my diary from several days after Donald's death until now. There was a vast silence inside me that terrified me with its power.

I had spent several weary weeks wishing for his death, and then suddenly, when confronted with his absence, I was unable to comprehend the enormity of what had happened. I spoke to the children through a sheet of glass, and longed for sleep that never came.

Temporary calm was replaced by disbelief. Then with the shock of acceptance, came an anxiety and anguish that I fear to write about, even now.

Friends spoke to me and I heard their voices, but not their thoughts. I shrank into a distant corner of my mind, as I tiptoed around the borders of insanity, trying to find my way back to the real world.

I am frightened by my own despair. I look at myself in the mirror and am fascinated by the lack of reflection. I see a figure, but no light, no movement, no expression. How strange to see such deadness in yourself.

When I was a little girl, we had a pair of doves nesting in our garden. For a couple of years, they pottered around the lawn together or sat on a branch in the camphor laurel tree and cooed at one another. My mother loved having them around. They suited the peaceful old garden very well.

One morning, a cat got the male bird and killed it. Confused and distraught, the little female trundled restlessly around the garden, calling and searching. We were all upset. It was horrible to watch. A few months later we found her lying dead under the magnolia bush, with no mark on her body. 'She died of a broken heart,' my mother announced.

Years later, Mum was describing to me the sadness and loneliness of her own widowhood, when suddenly she paused and whispered, 'Do you remember the little mother dove?'

Yes, I remember the mother dove. Even then, my childish perception told me that an unimaginably dreadful thing had happened to the little bird. I watched her searching and I knew that her loss was truly terrible.

Now, I think perhaps she was luckier than I. At least she had something to do: her compulsive trundling helped to pass the time. And she was spared the additional pain of real understanding of her loss.

I try not to envy the bird under the magnolia bush.

VII
A Brief Respite

• *1 December 1976* •

Tomorrow, I leave alone, at six a.m. for Sydney and then on to New Caledonia. Are you coming with me this time? Or are you away on dreams or journeys of your own? Where in this deep cosmic silence are you? My soul is cut adrift and wandering. Is there a port? Or is it a great empty nothing?

My bags are packed. Come away with me, my love, so that my heart may be at ease.

• *Vila* •

I flew from Noumea to the tiny island of Vila.

I have discovered the sad truth that your grief goes with you everywhere. It's the one piece of luggage that never gets lost on the journey. How I wish one of the many customs officers I have fronted up to, would pounce on it and say, 'Aha, you can't bring that in here. *Ce n'est pas possible.* You can pick that up on the way out.' Instead, it's like a serious physical deformity: it is part of you. The background music changes, that's all.

As the time expands, my perception and pain come creeping back again. Slowly it has dawned on me that I am truly alone, for the first time in my life.

• *Hideaway Island* •

I searched in the rock pools, quiet little worlds of their own, teeming with life that moves slowly, ponderously – life that is governed solely by the changing tides and the weather. I turned over a large shell and watched the small animal inside vomit up bright green seaweed in its effort to right itself again. Quickly I turned it over, regretting my intrusion on the remote world of the pool.

I found a band of the palest mauve shells clustered on a larger shell, looking for all the world like tiny fragile flowers. I had never seen anything quite like it and put it carefully back in the water.

• *Vila* •

I came to the New Hebrides in a daze. All the while I have been here, I have felt as though I am floating – just watching the scenery and looking at the people, without feeling anything. Donald took a long time to die. Unlike sudden or unexpected death, I had nearly nine months to anticipate my loss. I was well into my grieving long before he died and was forced to feel my pain in advance. Now that he is gone, my heart tells me to summon even more emotion. But I can't do it. I am emotionally dried out and will have to live in a vacuum for a while.

Very sadly I left Vila this morning. As I said goodbye to my favourite haunts on the island, I felt that I was also taking leave of a very special experience. I had found new strength and new courage while I was there and hope it will stay with me and give a new quality of peace and acceptance to familiar surroundings. My new acquaintance, Myra, who had come on a sentimental journey back to the place where she was born, was also feeling tearful when it came to leaving. I have been very grateful for the company of Myra and Geoff – Myra for her quick, warm sympathy, and Geoff for so courteously making me feel less of a widow.

The island is so beautiful. I wonder if I shall ever return? Even if I don't I will always be glad to have found my way to this peaceful corner of the world to nurse my unhappiness for a while.

VIII
Plenty of Black

• 20 December 1976 •
Canberra

Arriving home is a disaster. I feel as though I have been struck by lightning. I am giddy with pain.

There are so many reminders – the unfinished barbecue; the half-empty tin of tobacco; my Christmas present to you in the top of your wardrobe; the half-read book that will never be finished; the watch that was on your arm when you died; the other side of the bed – even the faces of my own children.

I think I am going mad.

• Friday Before Christmas •

The pain is indescribable. Every Friday is an anniversary of your death. Is it going to be like this all my life? Where does it end? I spend a whole week, carefully and secretly contemplating my own death. It would be so easy. I nursed the awesome prospect to myself. In a sense it was helpful. It gave me an alternative. Anything had to be an improvement on my present existence, even black, black nothingness.

I feel that I haven't tried long enough yet. You tried for eight long, weary months before you finally conceded defeat. The least I can do is equal that. But I mourn so.

I just went to the cellar to get a bottle of wine to add to Sue's Christmas basket, and my heart shattered all over again. You loved collecting those bottles. You sat crouching in the cellar for hours, cataloguing their contents. If only I could have you back for an hour, to feel your strong arms around me and to be still, to experience again the calm that your presence brought me.

With some shame and a great deal of sorrow, I have to admit that I did not know what my children were feeling during all this time. I didn't ask them. It was a time of solitary and terrifyingly selfish grieving that turned deeply inward.

After Donald died, we lost our lines of communication. The pattern of our lives seemed to diverge in every possible direction. This was probably my fault. Totally immersed in self-pity, I didn't think of asking them how they felt about it.

Later, as I calmed down and things became more normal, we started talking again . . . and were appalled by the loneliness we saw in each other.

Slowly, I felt the need to be a Mum instead of a bad tempered, disorganized harridan. Slowly, we became friends again. And in each one of them is a tremendous inner strength that arose out of their struggle to survive the death of Donald.

• *23 December* •

The car was red, my dress was red and my face was even redder. I had stalled the car for the third time in four days. It was the day before Christmas Eve and I had stopped in the middle of a busy intersection.

Rage and frustration fought with despair bordering on hysteria, as I strove to think clearly and decide what to do. Who to blame? How to make someone else look silly? I opened the boot, opened the bonnet, and turned on the hazard lights. With a bit of luck, everyone in the world would see that a two-year-old Volvo had broken down, and would decide not to buy one.

As I set off towards the nearest phone box, I reflected on the futility of my gesture. Tears started down my face, as I realized that this was yet one more indicator of my inability to control my unhappiness. Two previous warnings of a problem with the car had been ignored, and now I was in strife again. I felt unspeakably weary as I acknowledged the need to keep my daily life in better order.

Hug me. Oh, someone please hug me. I used to get such a lot of hugs once.

• *Christmas* •

I think of my first Christmas with Donald. Our first baby was due in a few weeks time, and you were so proud to be a husband and father. We celebrated with a quiet, brooding contentment, feeling even closer to the unborn child. We too, could see the star and feel for the little child of Bethlehem.

Following the tradition of our Danish forebears, we set aside Christmas Eve for our family festival. The children always stayed up late to watch the tree come to life. This time of year, above all others, reminded us of the miracle of our family life. We paused for a time and looked with wonder at the three little lives that had been placed in our care.

But this Christmas is different. All I can see is the harsh glitter of tinsel and tasteless baubles. All I can hear is the clatter of the cash registers. I am afraid to set the table for the feast. A place is empty and none of us can bear to turn our gaze to the empty chair. It is too soon. Our minds are fragile and torn with grief. This year the tree will not be lit.

I couldn't face Christmas. The carols and the gaiety seemed grotesque. For the first time in my life I physically abandoned the children, and went to Lilli Pilli with two perceptive friends. We stayed in a lovely house overlooking the water.

For ten days, I gratefully accepted their daily gift of caring. We lived quietly and in harmony as I sought release from my troubled mind. Christmas became a non-event. We just pretended it didn't happen.

Later, I was distressed to learn that Sue and Graeme spent Christmas day playing scrabble, trying to forget that Christmas is a family affair.

Maren went to Fraser Island, where she spent long, lazy weeks hiking and camping, dirty and dishevelled but happy. She deliberately blotted out the past few months and gave herself up to the sun and the sea and the wild loveliness of the island.

• *New Year's Eve* •

Tonight, we gathered at St Johns for the midnight service. It was a warm, velvety night and I sat on the old stone wall outside, and watched Sue in her long white gown, moving around the churchyard with her sleeping baby in her arms. Where were you? Did you see us confessing our sins from the year that was past and seeking absolution?

Right on midnight we knelt while the muffled bell tolled the old year out, and I whispered, 'Goodbye, my love. Let me go into the future.' The bell struck twelve and then the muffles were removed and the bells joyously welcomed in the new year. A new year and no Donald.

This is a stormy, difficult time. In fact, it seems to be the worst period of all. I have lost my sense of 'mission'. I no longer have a vigil to keep. I have seen to the estate and now have nothing to do except reflect on the magnitude of my loss.

It appears to be a totally destructive period but I think, in a harsh, violent way, it acts as a purge. I suffered in comparative silence for months and endured your death with complete calm. I think that all this self-discipline now has to be paid for in temporary loss of control. I rant and rage and find peace only when exhausted.

It nearly drives me mad, knowing my friends are waiting for a recovery that I feel may never come.

No one in the world ever came as close to sharing my vision as Donald. Our hearts whispered the same secrets, our eyes saw the same dreams and our souls curled up together to be at rest.

Even in his death, we saw our twinship. It was as though everything happened to both of us. He saw and experienced the pain of my coming loss and I looked with horror at his despair. Part of me seemed to die with him.

It's hard to share in such a departure without being drawn towards the vortex yourself. The way back seems so far. I wish I could paint a picture. I need to talk about things that can only be expressed in colour: there aren't enough words.

I need a huge canvas, and lots of red to paint heavy, sorrowing eyes, and black, plenty of black for the angry, screaming mouths. Sometimes there would be a yellow sun on still water, but mostly dark, threatening clouds crowding across the canvas and dwarfing the simple things.

And then, just as the painting seems settled and complete, the painter, livid with new pain, takes a knife and tears the canvas to shreds and starts again.

Maren was at university in Armidale the year her father was ill. She sat for her final exams a few days before Donald died. Now, she has been offered a job at ANU.

She is still fretting, poor little soul, and was very tearful tonight, because normally we would all sit down and talk about her future. Her grief is much more real to her since she came home. She, too, is noticing the empty chair.

In one sense, we're grateful that we care so much and miss him so terribly. In another sense, we are frantic with silence and emptiness.

We both agree that the pain must be much worse for Graeme, who insists on suffering in silence. I found a card he had written to Donald in hospital. It said 'I want to wish you a happy fiftieth birthday tomorrow. Do you realize that there are lots of people around who are twice your age?' Poor kid. Right up to the end, he kept saying 'It won't happen.' But it did.

Because you said he could, Graeme bought a car for twenty dollars. Such lunacy and idiotic irresponsibility left me speechless. Why did we have to have a useless rusty old wreck cluttering up the backyard? Why did I have to endure this extra, totally unnecessary irritation? Well, as so often before, it was because of your understanding of the needs of this male child, whose interests only baffled and frustrated me.

Carefully and lovingly he stripped it down and cleaned, polished, and repaired. Then equally painstakingly, he reassembled it and painted the towbar purple. And so the long summer passed, and when the time came for first semester, the little car carried him slowly but faithfully across the city each day, and in doing so brought great comfort to its owner. Apparently layers and layers of engine oil and sticky black grease have therapeutic value that entirely escapes me. Men! I never will understand.

Why is it that when I lose weight my hips retain their over-lavish, pear-shaped contours, while my face develops cracks wide enough to drive a truck through?

And my hair. My hairdresser seems to have resurrected that depressing shade of grey she tried unsuccessfully once before.

The oil bill came today.

I have decided to send Donald's clothes to the Smith family. Goodness knows what they'll do with all these size 13 shoes and suits for a broad shouldered man of 6′3″. But that's their problem.

Graeme sat on the bed and watched as I sorted and packed. Occasionally I paused to smell the tweed of a jacket or smooth the wrinkles in his old cords. His presence lingers in the fabric.

I held up a fawn suit, freshly dry cleaned and ready to wear. Graeme stirred uneasily and said 'Let's keep that one to remind us how big he was.' I shoved my head in the wardrobe to hide my tears from him.

• *February* •

It's funny how quickly officialdom has moved in to clear away the remnants of our marriage. Computers, normally slow to accept changes of address, have shown amazing speed in converting Mrs D. V. MacDonald to Mrs B. A. MacDonald. Even Telecom has marked me down as a widow.

I nearly burst into tears in front of everyone in the bank

when I was handed my first 'widowed' cheque book. Not being very liberated, I had always felt that our two names looked rather sweet snuggling together at the bottom of our cheques. Whereas my own name by itself looks weak and fragile and incapable of standing alone.

Intellectually, I know that none of this is true. I know that some marvellously efficient and far thinking person has moved in and spared me the worry of attending to these details myself. It's just that I feel as though even the prime minister has drawn a thick black line through Donald's name and written 'widow' beside my own.

There are twenty-two ladybirds on the tea-towel, all crawling in the same direction. Why did I count them, for heaven's sake? I don't know . . . it seemed to have as much point as anything else I do these days.

Everything is smothered in a vast blanket of boredom that renders every action uniform in its effect. I used to live on a marvellous 'Big Dipper'. Some days were fantastic and some were terrible. But never this sameness.

Graeme and his mates have erected a pulley in the roof of our garage, so they can mend their lousy old wrecks of cars at our place.

Why me, I ask myself? Why do I have to wash all the coffee mugs and clean the grease spots off the carpet?

Well actually, I do enjoy hearing their friendly banter and loud guffaws. He keeps me at a safe distance. I'm too sad for him. He needs his cheerful friends, and escapes with obvious relief for long hours at a stretch. I feel completely isolated from them but I'm glad they come.

About six months ago, Donald bought me a length of heavenly blue chiffon.

'Have it made into something really special,' he urged. 'The colour suits you, and I do so want you to go on looking good.'

For a long time it lay hidden in the back of my wardrobe, a traitor to my mood. When he died, I vowed I would never attend another opera. Now, three months later, the new gown hangs in my wardrobe, ready to wear to the opening night of *Madame Butterfly*.

This isn't because I have forgotten my vow or ceased to care. I must bring fresh life to the part of me that always responded so deeply to this musical feast. Never let it be said that my spirit starved for the want of good music.

'Excuse me. Didn't you go to school at North Sydney High?'

It was a hot sultry morning in February and we were both standing outside the petrol station, waiting for our cars to be filled. I looked uncertainly at the dark, slim woman in front of me.

'I was Lorna W–.'

Then I remembered. We had been at school together since we were seven and hadn't met since the hot, carefree day in 1946 when we said goodbye to the old school for the last time. We had parted with such high expectations and enthusiasm for the future.

I looked at Lorna and my eyes filled with tears as I remembered our girlish exuberance. Life was so full of promise and the way ahead seemed so clear and inviting. I explained briefly that my husband had just died and we hastily exchanged addresses. I promptly lost Lorna's and she mislaid mine.

This chance meeting was followed by a separate grief. I longed to tell her how happy I had been. I wanted to explain it hadn't all ended in death, that there were three wonderful children who still brought a different happiness into my life. I wanted to tell her about my best friend who had shared my life for twenty-three wonderful years.

Much later, we met again and have since laughed and cried together as we talked of the years we shared as little girls at school, and the years we didn't share, moving into our separate futures.

The pain I feel now is greatly increased by the happiness I felt before. In the same way, I feel that any happiness I experience in the future will be more golden because of the pain I carry with me now. Sometimes, this gives me a greater serenity and deeper tranquility than I have ever felt before. I'm learning to live without Donald and there's a place inside me that is gentle and quiet and calm, in spite of the outward ranting and raging.

'Mary, it's too hard. It wasn't worth it. Nothing is worth all this pain. I just can't keep going like this.'

'But you said last week that you were feeling better.'

'Well, I was lying. I'm not. I'm worse than ever. Oh Mary, try not to love Bob too much. It's just too damned hard.'

Mary has unusually beautiful grey eyes and as I said this, they swam with tears that ran unchecked down her face and splashed onto the papers on her desk.

'But sometimes you feel better,' she pleaded. 'You're not unhappy all the time.'

My catastrophic ups and downs never cease to amaze me. How did the bird under the magnolia engineer her own death? How come I'm still breathing when there's nothing left to breathe for?

Time passes. It does you know, even as they say it does. I used to think they were rotten liars and their soft words were only a conspiracy to stop me from cutting my throat. But they're not. Imperceptibly, the pain grows duller and I don't feel so bleak. I'm not suggesting that suddenly it's a bed of roses. But time does pass.

I told my mother today. Why did I tell her? Because her first question was, 'Where is Donald?' You see, we always visited together. He was the comedian of the nursing home and they all enjoyed his company. I started to say, 'Mum, Donald has been very ill . . .' But as her eyes searched my face for the truth, it all bubbled out. 'Oh Mum, Mum, he died.'

'Oh no, not Donald,' she crooned, 'Not Donald. It couldn't be Donald. He loved everything so much. How did you stay sane?'

Gently, I explained it all to her and dried her tears. You might well ask why I did tell her? Why did I have to pull her out of senile amnesia to participate in my grief? She is my mother.

My earliest memory of grief was when the daily newspapers revealed the full horror of the German concentration camps.

My war had been a fairly distant thing. I was still at school and it seemed a long way away. My father was in a high-security occupation and my brother returned safely from his stint in the navy.

On the day the war ended in Europe, the senior school was summoned to the assembly hall. I watched in open mouthed disbelief as I saw some of the toughest cookies in the teaching profession weeping openly and unashamedly. Somehow, I still hadn't fully understood.

Then the allied armies reached the concentration camps

and the horror spread like a palpable mass over the whole civilized world. Each day's news reported a crescendo of human bestiality that surely would never be equalled in the history of the world. But no, the reports on the following day would sink to an even greater depth of horror and degradation. And every night, I cried myself to sleep. It seemed grotesque that my own youth had been so peaceful and uneventful, while millions of innocent souls endured, or failed to endure, the combined hells of Belsen, Auschwitz, and Treblinka.

I have since read that the birds, insects, and small animals have never returned to the earth around Belsen. A common instinct has warned them that this piece of God's earth has been branded for all time.

I still have a deep abiding sorrow for the suffering and loss of the Jewish people during those ghastly years. By comparison, my present grief seems clean and wholesome and easier to understand. The loss is easier to accept.

IX
New Beginnings

• *February 1977* •

Tonight, I took Anne to dinner in the Garden Court at the Wentworth. As we walked through the door, we were enfolded by the navy blue walls and the quiet, opulent charm of the large dining room. The table was crisply white with a single red rose in the centre, offsetting the sparkle of the crystal and silver. Outside, the willows swayed and bent in a pale green dance of their own.

Our waiter was a charming, dark-eyed Italian who made us feel a million dollars. The food was good, and the setting was delightful. There was much to enjoy. Even so, when the waiter said to Anne, 'Your friend is enjoying herself very, very much, is she not?' I was surprised and even, I suspect, faintly shocked. It hardly seemed decent to be so obviously happy.

I wonder how much of my present happiness is an attempt to counterbalance the pure horror of last year? Perhaps those weary painful days have left me with a greater perception of joy when it comes. The contrast is increasingly evident in my capacity to laugh and inhale pleasure.

Slowly, ever so slowly, it has become a challenge to make other people laugh. The other day I realized with a shock that my thoughts have been turned inwards for so long that I no longer care how others are faring. My problems have dominated every waking hour. My work is a drudge, my children are just there, and everything else is a dreary bore.

Relinquishing this immense self-pity, and returning to the real world of human relationships, is the biggest single step I have to take. It's painful too, because with it comes the realization that everyone else's suffering is greatly enlarged in my mind. I have acquired a capacity to understand the people around me to a degree I have not experienced before.

• *March* •

It was raining this morning as I thumbed through the paper with the pessimistic interest of one who was in tune with the weather. Quite unexpectedly, my eyes lit on an advertizement for a tiny split-level townhouse in a very attractive development at Urambi Village on the outskirts of Canberra. As it happened, I had some insurance of Donald's that was in need of safe investment. Have you ever noticed how freely you spend money when you are unhappy?

The more I thought about it, the more the idea of buying it appealed to me. Finally I decided to go out and have a look for myself. As I passed through the dining room, the children glanced up briefly from a game of scrabble to ask where I was going.

'To buy a townhouse,' I replied. Hoots of derision and laughter all round.

The rain pelted down as I drove around the development. The whole area was a sloppy, repulsive mess. However, I was in the mood to buy and was not easily diverted. It took me all of ten minutes to decide on Number 65 and pay the necessary deposit. All that remained was to convince my bank manager of the economic brilliance of the scheme.

As I walked back through the dining room, the kids looked up with a yawn and said, 'Where have you been?'

'To buy a townhouse.'

'Oh yes . . .'

I smiled and silently hugged my secret to myself.

This has been a strange day. In buying Urambi, I am buying back my own future. It's mine, all mine. Buying this little house is an acknowledgement that the future not only exists, but is desirable and worth planning for. It takes into account the fact that one day, all the children will have left home and I shall no longer need a rambling two-storey house designed for family living. Long before this happens, I have selected a dwelling that suits my individual requirements.

Meanwhile, I can see a degree of flexibility that could be difficult to achieve otherwise. I hope my bank manager sees it the same way.

• *April* •

Bank managers have always scared me to death. Personally I believe they are specially trained to terrify their victims. I still remember how mortified I felt when, aged twenty-four, I arrived at the bank clutching the mortgage documents for our new home, only to be sent back to fetch my husband. This was particularly irritating because Donald never displayed the slightest interest in our financial affairs. In fact, he had a decided aversion to bank statements and was more than happy to leave our wobbly budget to me.

Later, as the grey crept into my hair and our finances improved, bank managers became markedly more civil and more inclined to listen to my chatter about the state of our economy.

Now, even when my hairdresser has made a better than usual attempt to hide the grey, they tend to be very polite. All the same, I am scared stupid by the prospect of fronting up, and defending and justifying my townhouse.

My appointment with the bank manager was for eleven a.m. I was very nervous, not even sure that I was doing the right thing. As I walked through the Plaza, a flock of tiny birds flew past in perfect formation, with all the ceremony of an airforce 'fly-past'. Laughing at their salute, I straightened up and determined not to make a complete idiot of myself.

The interview went like a dream. To start with, he was a very nice man. I had planned what I wanted to say carefully and had all the figures I needed in front of me. I explained the project and told him how I wanted the whole exercise to be a progressive one with escape clauses at each point. He said it was the best interview he had had in years, had I ever considered a career in banking?

The result was that he offered me the full sum I asked for and approved it on the spot. I just couldn't believe it. I walked back through the Plaza feeling ten feet tall.

• *May* •

There must be a period of numbness immediately after the death of someone close to you. At first, I was surprised and impressed by my calm acceptance. While I organized the funeral, I was amazed at the way I talked and chatted and seemed to take everything in my stride. It was incredibly simple, even for an emotional drop-out like me.

Now the scene has changed. I am bitter and angry and horrifyingly out of control. I'm angry with my staff and cruel to my friends. It's a wonder I still have any. I rarely miss an opportunity to make an unkind or poisonous remark. I have taken to writing letters that are carefully calculated to be devastating to the recipients. I seem to have acquired a positive genius for writing things that will cause deep and lasting wounds.

One of the worst was aimed at Mary, who has had the gall to go on being happy when I am slowly disintegrating with grief. Mercifully, she saw through my pain and chose to ignore it. I wrangle with tradesmen and shout at the kids. My lack of control is positively obscene. Even the poor, defenceless old dog isn't immune from my onslaught. She skulks around the house looking dejected and trying not to be noticed. Her 'mother' has suddenly and unaccountably taken leave of her senses; cuddles are a thing of the past.

Probably the person who is suffering most is poor old Graeme, who is a readily available target. I don't even seem to care if his heart is hurting, except in the wee, small hours of the morning when I long to put my arms around him and tell him I'm sorry.

There are days when I sit in the toilet for half an hour at a stretch and howl. It's surprising how, if you really put your mind to it, you can find hourly fault with everything that happens. Black is a good colour and misery my best friend. Don't talk to me about yellow. I don't want to know.

'Shall I play for you?'

'Yes, please do. I would really love that.'

'I make an awful lot of mistakes but you won't mind, will you?'

Curled up in a large armchair, I shared Mary's sweet mood as her fingers moved across the keyboard. Her own happiness reached out to me and caressed my sadness, begging it to be still.

Around midnight, I left for home, feeling calmer and saner than I had felt for a long time.

Last night, I dreamt it was Sunday and Donald was making me breakfast in bed. I woke up to find it's Monday and Donald no longer exists.

This time last year, I was so afraid he would die in the

autumn or the winter. I would listen to the currawongs calling, and wonder if they were calling him. There was no message of hope in their cry. It would have been so sad and somehow incongruous if his life had ended with the closing of the season. I longed to be able to say just once more, 'Look darling, there's a crocus and the daffodils are in bud.'

Beginnings are terribly important to me – even, then, the beginning of his death. Had I been consulted by the Divine Majesty who plans these things, I would have said, 'Let it be after the spring.' So it was.

• *June* •

I sat in the swinging chair at Urambi today and marvelled at the peace I found there. I shall always remember this place with gratitude. The house is almost complete. There are only the curtains to go up, and Ian has agreed to finish the landscaping in the next week or so.

It has been a marvel of achievement for me. I planned the whole project from beginning to end, and I did it alone. There have been times when I have doubted, but now it has worked well. I even have a tenant for the next twelve months.

Yesterday, Maren planted trees and I spread tanbark out the front. Graeme has put a shiny brass '65' on the door. It's my own little house.

Don Giovanni. So many painful things are now safely embedded in my subconscious mind. I make no effort to bring them out and by and large they are content to stay there. But that one aria from *Don Giovanni* – oh my darling, I can hear your voice as though it were yesterday. I loved it so much. And thank God, I always knew how much. At least I don't grieve for opportunities lost of telling you.

But now, I'm lonely. In the midst of all these friends and family, I'm unbelievably, unbearably lonely. I sometimes wonder whether the heaviest part of my grief is brought on by my not having a sufficient outlet for the love I felt for you. My love goes out to the children in a steady stream, but then, it always did. This other love was something separate that was only shared by the two of us.

What an ugly word grief is. When will it go away?

The little finches are in the courtyard as never before. I watched them bathing in the pool.

• *July* •

It's another Friday night, but nearly seven months further on. So long? Where did I find the strength? I held you as you died. My God, why didn't I scream and go insane?

I was talking to Mary the other day about how important those last eight months were to both of us. We had spent a long time falling in love, and we needed a long time to say goodbye. In fact, we seemed to need every minute, except during those last two weeks. And perhaps even they served a purpose in showing me how impossible it was for your soul to continue to inhabit your poor, useless body. When I think of our farewell, it is always to the song of the currawongs.

It was almost like our lovemaking – unhurried, and so very, very tender. For nearly eight months, we said goodbye. We reminisced about a past we had shared and we planned a future that would not hold you.

• *October* •

This afternoon I bought a dear little wooden trike for Edward's first birthday. Graeme and I have been riding it around the dining room for the last hour or so.

When I was up at the hospital the other day, I talked to

one of the sisters who nursed Donald, and she asked after Edward. She said 'You know, I happened to come into the room just as your daughter placed the baby in your arms for the first time. I have never seen anything quite like the smile on your face as you held him and I thought to myself, she'll be all right. Then I saw Mr MacDonald watching you, with tears running down his face and I had to leave the room to hide my own tears. I shall never forget that moment as long as I live.'

My kids are having a wonderful time helping to rear our toy baby. It's just as well he has a strong personality of his own. He seems to adore his collection of interfering relatives.

This is an extract from a letter from Mary's grandmother, eighty years old. Most of it's not true. But I wonder if you can understand how much this letter means to me and how incredibly supportive it is:

'Because this is nearly the first anniversary of your great sorrow, I feel I must write just a short note to say I'm thinking of you and praying that God will give you the strength to cope with it all. You are very brave. I think you have a ton of courage. I know how hard it is for you, my dear, but you will continue to grow stronger. Your family will bring you great joy and so will your home and your beautiful garden. So be happy, my dear . . . be very, very happy.'

I have never felt such a need for encouragement and support and good old-fashioned back slapping as I do now. When Donald died my mirror broke and I no longer saw a reflection of my own performance.

Every little effort on the part of the bereaved deserves disproportionate praise and encouragement. Unless you have been through it, you cannot even begin to know how hard it is. A whole new self-image has to be constructed and it's a lonely and difficult task.

You might well ask if it was worth it. Did the joy of the first twenty years make up for the pain and unhappiness of this past twelve months? The answer would have to be yes. I count myself as truly blessed in every sense of the word. I have lived joyously, and I have suffered hideously. But through it all has been a richness that I cannot find words to describe. My whole life has been altered and deepened by the journey I took beside this man I loved and the children he gave me. And now, although he no longer shares my existence, he has left in me an abiding contentment with the life I continue to pursue.

Sometimes the children nearly drive me mad. Although ostensibly grown up, they seem to make an awful lot of noise and create their own special brand of havoc around the house. They leave a trail of books, papers, records, underwear, and coffee mugs everywhere they go. I don't really vacuum upstairs. I just sort of poke the vacuum cleaner at any odd pieces of carpet that show through. However, when the debris starts to spread down to the ground floor, I line it up on the staircase where they'll fall over it, on their way up. The playroom looks like a badly organized junkshop.

Even so, my heart stands still at the thought of the silence that will descend when they have gone.

• *6 November* •

It is twelve months today since we said goodbye. It seems so much longer. Perhaps the weariness of the solitary journey has made it seem so: stumbling, despairing, sometimes almost giving up. They say the first twelve months are the worst. I hope so. It's so exhausting to struggle so hard. It's not even a nine to five occupation. It seems to cover twenty-four hours a day, seven days a week.

And yet, the struggle has been worth it. There is a soft, sweet sadness inside me that will never disappear, but side by side with the sadness is a sense of warmth and well-being that cannot be denied. Indeed it is enhanced by this awful journey we took together.

If any of you are on this journey now, take hold of every moment and treasure it and make it as beautiful as you can. Let your tears flow, but let them flow together. Share your love and your memories, and even dare to think about the future.

• *November* •

The waterlilies in the pond are in full flower. The Egyptian lotus was a waterlily, as was the sacred lotus of the Hindus. According to ancient legend, the lotus flower was offered to Ulysses and his men during their travels. If they ate it, they would forget family and friends and want to remain forever on the island.

Gazing into the heart of these perfect but ancient flowers, with their curved, waxy petals and golden stamen, I forget everything and find peace of mind.

Slowly my grief has taken on a mellowness that makes it bearable. A lightness steals into my heart that whispers to me of wholeness and recovery. The future is veiled in uncertainty, and there are many question marks in my mind. I am still plagued by a considerable degree of laziness and inertia.

And yet, I cannot deny a languid stretching out towards the sun. Life is worth living and I am slowly learning to enjoy myself in a different, more independent way.

Contact with friends I knew before I met Donald has

convinced me that I am still basically a whole person. I prefer to think of myself not as a widow, but as a woman with lots of warmth and laughter spilling over into other people's lives.

I have chosen to keep on walking. My sorrow is no longer the major element of my existence. It has become a sombre thread in the pattern of my life, blending with the other, brighter threads.

The garden in the courtyard could best be described as a barely controlled jungle. Sometimes I marvel that the same flowers keep on flowering and the same trees come into bloom. Why didn't the apricot rose die of grief? I nearly did. Why do the currawongs keep coming back to a garden so bereft?

But it's comforting to know that these things are constant. They all help in the healing of the human spirit.

• *January 1978* •

I have come back to the beach where we spent our last holiday. When it was first suggested that I should join Anne and her family for Christmas, I was very dubious. It sounded like an unnecessarily painful experience. Besides, I might find that my memory of it was all a dream, a fabrication.

In my darkest moments, I have often wondered whether we were really as happy as I thought we were. Perhaps it was a figment of my imagination, a sort of compensating mechanism. Perhaps it was a very ordinary marriage, really.

This morning, I got up about five and saw that soft pink was beginning to stain the sky. I pulled on some clothes and went down to the beach. Incredibly, the same rocks were standing, staring out to sea, just as they were when you shared my view.

As I stood with the water washing quietly over my feet, I felt again the pure joy of the love I had known. There was no pain, just warm, pale pink pleasure. Oh my love, we were happy, you and I. You made life so beautiful for me. God forgive me, if I sometimes scream with the anguish of having lost you.

This holiday is proving to be marvellously therapeutic. I seem to need to spend a lot of time on my own, reading, swimming, or just thinking. But Anne and Garth and the boys are always there when I need company. We usually have dinner together and afterwards go for a long, long walk over the rocks and along the beach. Very gently, and with immense perception, they are teaching me how to relate to another married couple without pain. They are putting the strands of their friendship back into my hands and saying, 'Here you are. We were here all the time, but you weren't listening. Now take hold again. We need you too.' Warm, funny, and friendly, they are marvellous.

The tan on my skin is deepening and the scorch marks on my soul are fading. I'm beginning to see the faint outline of a person I might recognize as my new self, though it's still rather blurry. She has a heart. My goodness, she has a heart. And a brain, that's slowly beginning to work again. And she has eyes, eyes that grew weary of looking at the dark silence on all sides. Now, those eyes are awash with the colour of petunias in the park, the white of the seagulls on the crisp new sand, and the sweet repose of the sunset over the land, as the sky darkens into night. Do you know, there were times when I didn't even see the stars in their frail loveliness. My pain must have been very bad indeed.

Scott, Anne's younger son, had often told me there was a lovely path along the cliff-top. Every evening, he ran along the cliffs by himself, feeling good after a long day in the sun and surf.

This afternoon, I decided to look for it myself. It was a wonderful feeling being alone and distant, high up above the world.

As I rounded a bend and came to an opening in the thick undergrowth, I was stunned by the scene that was spread out before me. It had waited for me. It had waited all that time, for me to come back.

Far below, a fisherman was standing well out on an overhanging rock. The sea was deep and threatening below him, but he was totally absorbed in his fishing and at peace with the world.

Tears stung my eyes as I looked again at the scene we had been watching when we talked about our holiday in Greece. We had taken a picnic around the cliff-tops and stretched out in the sun, in this exact spot. You promised me we would go to Greece together. You held my hand and smiled, as you talked about the years that lay ahead of us. But you didn't tell me about the storm that would engulf us before I would see the fisherman on the rock again.

• *February* •

The children have a two-string kite – a great big blue one. Graeme gave it to Sue for her twenty-third birthday because *he* wanted one. I suppose I should be flattered that they invited me to join them on Capitol Hill for the grand launching. It has been a very windy day and they had a marvellous time. Children, friends, baby and dog were all muddled up with wet nappies, kite strings, and overcoats. Edward's nappies fell off in the excitement and he ran on, naked and absorbed with the new toy. I made lots of kites when I was a little girl, but none of them ever flew. I wish I had gone up with this one. Kites have a life of their own, as they ride the wind, away from all human caring.

• *March* •

This morning I went looking for a birthday card for Mary. I inadvertently picked up the sweetest card with two little mice cuddled up together. When I opened it up, it said, 'Happy Anniversary'. Before I had time to put it down, big tears had splashed all over the picture. So I put it right at the back and hurried away.

Today, I need to bury my face in the fawn suit and cry and cry and cry . . . joining my sorrow with the despair of the world, in this day's grief. Some days are still dressed in sober grey. Perhaps a time will never come when the sun shines every day.

It's hard to distinguish between grief and self pity. Where does one leave off and the other begin? I mean, how much of my grieving is because Donald has gone and how much because I am alone and wallowing in fear of the future?

When should I let myself be, and when should I say: 'Enough! Leave off. You said all that before. Don't be so boring. Go and make some biscuits. Do something for someone else, but stop boring me with all that pain. Tell me about sunshine and Smarties and rainbows. Tell me that plants still grow and birds still sing and little babies smile at their mothers for the first time.'

• *April* •

I was given a secret and unexpected gift this morning. I went into the city and found the trees had turned corn yellow when I wasn't looking. The sober green of summer had been swept away, and the city sparkled and shone with its newfound gold.

The autumn in Canberra seems to be different from anywhere else in the world. Most cities look rather forlorn as they watch the approaching winter. But Canberra shines with a new life and takes on a quality of tenderness that coaxes you to walk slowly and experience the season to the full.

• *June* •

After she graduated, Maren worked for two years to save enough money to travel around Europe on her pushbike. She planned meticulously, even selling her collection of shells to help pay her fare. With a mixture of excitement and prolonged panic, she resigned from her job and set out on her journey. Still longing to see Greece, I have arranged to meet her in Athens.

• *Athens* •

It is blisteringly hot in Athens, with heat bouncing off the pavement and scorching my eyes. And the YWCA in the centre of the city isn't exactly my palace of dreams.

• *July* •
Nauplion

Wearying of the noise and heat of Athens, we took a boat to the seaside town of Nauplion. This is my gift to Maren before she begins the hardships of budget travel on her bicycle.

It's hard to believe we have already been here more than a week. We sit mesmerized by the landscape.

Bottomless depths of turquoise sea. Maren swimming with fair hair streaming behind her. Jacarandas mauve against a blue lacquered sky.

Lazing under a red umbrella sharing *The Times*, a Greek salad and a glass of lemon. Sitting by the water staring at the endless horizon.

Solid harshness of the interior with the sun beating down on the olive groves and the brutal, rocky landscape.

Amethyst hills around the still water with the cool of the evening stealing the light from the sky.

Will I remember this?

One day, we made our way up the hill to the ancient stone fortress that dominates the township. Right in the heart of the fort, we came across a little stone chapel. Inside, we found a pile of slender candles for departed souls. Without a word, we lit two candles for our own dearly loved departed soul. We were both misty-eyed as we went back into the sunlight, leaving our candles burning in the sand.

As evening fell, we caught a bus to the ancient theatre of Epidaurus. We took our tea with us and sat in the ruins of the Temple of Asclepius absorbing the atmosphere of the silently brooding stones. The world seemed to stand still and wait for eternity.

As night crept over the hills, we made our way slowly up to the theatre, where as part of the Festival of Epidaurus, we were to see Sophocles' *Electra*, performed by the Greek Drama Company. It is an awesome thought that people like us were seated on that same circle of stones, listening to the same plays, as long as two thousand years ago.

I found it easy to follow and was intensely moved by the

simple drama, set against a stark grey backdrop. The standing ovation that followed the last act seemed barely adequate to express our sense of privilege for having been there.

• August •
Athens

Although I didn't come to Greece with Donald, it has proved to be an intensely satisfying experience. I don't feel closer to him, as I had half expected. Somehow, he seems even further away than before. These are people and places I have never shared with him, and this seems to make it easier. For a while, I no longer feel that constant sense of absence and amputation. This whole new experience is Maren's and mine. The memories of Donald are back in Australia.

In the morning, we fly to London and soon I shall be leaving for home.

X
The Colours are Beautiful Now

• August 1978 •
Canberra

It's indescribably wonderful to be home – to sink back into the familiar comfort and just float through the hours. Here is a place where I speak the language, know the currency and have full board forever and ever. Here is a place where my friends know where to find me and the children call me Mum.

It has been the longest journey of my life. A journey I had expected Donald to take with me. Instead, it proved to be a voyage of discovery in every sense of the word.

I learnt not to cry as I sat alone in a tea shop, stirring my tea and pretending not to care. I learnt to enjoy doing things that had nothing to do with Donald. I lost some of my compulsion to tug at people's coat tails and say, 'Hey, I had this fantastic friend . . . but he died.'

My life is so different from the dreams I once held. So different from the way we had planned it together. And yet, over all, is a deep, deep calm and intense happiness. If you had told me this, back in those dark, despairing days after he died, I would never have believed you. I had to learn for myself that the world throbs with a beauty and harmony that bids you go on.

I have mixed bowls of flowers all over the house.

The other night we watched the funeral of a local dignitary on TV and there were no flowers. So I turned to the kids and said, 'Let's get this straight. When I die, there's to be none of this nonsense about "no flowers by request". You're to put a notice in the paper saying: "Please bring big bunches of flowers, by special request of the deceased."'

Maren sent me a present. It was a sponge she found on the beach in Crete, an affordable memento of the time she spent there, picking avocados and oranges.

I love it. It's like a magic carpet. Each morning as I lather up, I dream about the sun coming up in Spetsai and the deep beautiful blue of the Aegean. Even on a rainy day in Canberra, I can feel the hot, dry heat of Athens on my back and hear the voices of the sponge-sellers in the street.

• *20 March 1979* •

This would have been our silver wedding anniversary. Riddled with fresh pain, I have hidden myself away from the world for the day. I don't want to share this very special grief. No one knows where I am and no one has guessed that I am quietly raising my glass to what might have been. Even so, I have to acknowledge that this is a kind of pain that I seldom experience any more. My grief has resolved itself into a quiet calm, that brings with it enormous strength.

There are nice things about winter. Returning along the dark, icy roads, knowing there will be a warmly lit home at the end of your journey. To open the door, and be greeted by the smell of thick, hot soup. To exchange your work clothes for a long woolly dressing gown and a pair of old socks. And then when all else has been done, to close the door and turn out the light and snuggle under your doona, with only your nose aware of the bitter cold outside.

The candlelight flickers softly on the flowers in the centre of the table and lights up the young faces gathered around me. The place at the head of the table is no longer empty. Graeme, our youngest child, has long since taken your place, first hesitantly, and then with all the confidence of a young man who knows where he's going.

Sue wears her motherhood with an easy grace. Her baby has grown into a handsome and loveable three-year-old. Soon, he will be joined by another baby. Maren has returned safely from her journeys around Europe on a pushbike.

It is nearly three years since you left us. We talk of you often. We share our memories with pain and delight. We are proud to have known you, darling, and grateful to have shared for a time your journey through life.

Tonight there is a fierce electrical storm in the air. The thunder is shouting around the skies and the night is a deep, thick blue, promising intimacy and warmth.

The cat is curled up on the end of my bed and we looked at each other as we shared the softness of the rain in the courtyard. It's a lovely night.

I think somebody has opened me up and sewn my laugh back in. What a miracle! Living is so much easier when it's funny.

• *May 1981* •

Graeme, the baby of the family, graduated today. Is it possible that we have come so far?

I felt a terrible need to share this happening with you, my love. It seemed only fair that you should share my pride. The long-haired boy with the felt hat and the knees out of his jeans has finished being a boy and is stepping into a man's world.

As the procession began, the orchestra played . . . of all things . . . 'Praise my soul the King of Heaven'. The music we sang at our wedding. Is it any wonder I cried a little? But oh darling, I was so proud of the tall boy with the long hair in his purple gown.

He was late, of course. His clapped-out old car broke down three times on the way down from Sydney. His name was called twice before he appeared breathless and dishevelled on the platform. But he made it, darling, even as you always said he would. And I was so proud.

Donald and I always did our best fighting outdoors. Preferably in the middle of the front lawn where we could be sure of a good audience. None of this mumbling in the bedroom for us. If we were having a row, we liked to broadcast it around the neighbourhood.

And what was the cause of the arguments? The most inconsequential things you could possibly imagine.

'You can't grow roses on my bean fence.'

'Who says wattles won't grow in New Zealand?' In fact, there are veritable groves of them wherever we lived, still lending their golden spring to the landscape.

One of our loudest arguments centred on the planting of the almond tree.

'Almonds won't grow in Canberra. Besides, I want a flowering cherry there.' Because he was bigger than me and could actually dig the hole in the hard, unyielding clay, he won. He planted the almond tree. I sniggered as I watched the leafless stick struggle for life. Clearly it was not happy.

Then one frosty morning two years later, just as winter ended, it was covered in huge, white sweetly scented flowers. The bees were in abundance and in the summer we gathered our first nuts.

This morning, I crunched across the frosty lawn to pick up the newspaper and was greeted by a burst of pure white blossom reaching towards the sky. Their coming is always a surprise and their greeting reassuring. You see . . . he left me the almond tree.

Graeme's old car has finally given up the ghost. Even he has to admit that it's not a viable form of transport anymore.

Reluctantly, he sold it for parts and this morning called a truck to tow it away. We stood at the kitchen window watching it slowly inch its way up the drive. Somehow, I felt as though part of our life's experience was going with it.

As we turned away, he saw that I was crying and seemed grateful for the understanding. We've come a long way, he and I.

Mary, who is tired of pharmacology and wants to be a fashion designer made me a magic jacket. One side is ruby red paisleys with red velvet trimming. That's the side I wear when I go shopping. The other side is deep blue velvet outlined in red. That's the side I wear to the Opera. Sometimes, I change it over at interval.

We spent hours crawling around on the floor in David Jones selecting the fabrics; so much of both of us went into the choosing.

I never go away without it. It brings a sense of home to any awful old orange and brown motel. It's a totally forgiving garment. No matter what I do, it still comes up smiling.

And the strange thing is that whenever I wear it, people smile at me. The most unlikely people are distracted from their gloom and grin happily at the sight of the ageing pixie in her red jacket. I tell you it's magic.

Last night, I found a big daddy-long-legs in the bathroom. He was in danger of being washed down the plug hole. So I carefully put him on the bench where he sat and solemnly waved his feelers at me. I felt very involved with him and talked to him for some time.

Late at night, I found him struggling on his back on the carpet. I picked him up again. He seemed weary and confused.

Tonight, he was dead in the soap dish. His small body was quite empty of life. Such a brief passing and yet he seemed important to me.

I laid the little wisp of fine legs in the ferns, and wondered. Did his life just go out like a candle? Was that all there was for him?

• September 1984 •
To Georgie, the Golden Labrador

Today, little dog, I buried your collar. Because I wasn't here when you died, I needed to do something. You were my last link with our old life. I dug a hole in your favourite piece of garden, where you always trod on the petunias.

I sat in the dirt with the worn leather in my hand and marvelled at the way you took over our lives. How did such a tiny bundle of cream fluff become such a force in our household?

Yesterday, I walked through 'the hundred acre wood' where Donald and I used to take you and the children on a Sunday afternoon. There was a quiet nostalgia in the place where we once walked.

The ground was damp and soggy and wild roses caught my skirt. There was a rabbit, and two cranky magpies. You would have loved it.

It was a bit lonely without you. I kept turning around to call and just as I thought I saw a flash of cream fur, I remembered . . .

Now I'm going back into the garden to plant a tree. I shall pat the earth down carefully and sit on the ground for a while and think about you and me and Dad and all the kids. So long, Georgie.

Lots of people when widowed or divorced, feel they will never be whole again unless they remarry. There are times when I have unconsciously agreed. Certainly that deep and intimate friendship has been the greatest loss of my life. Even now, I would dearly love to have that one close friend who makes you feel so special.

But when I was surrounded by a busy and growing family, much of life's hidden meaning passed me by. I simply didn't have time to notice. Now that I'm alone I have time to pause and listen for the heartbeats of others and try harder to understand what their life means to them. Even my own children spring into a different dimension and become adults whose lives are truly separate from my own. I still ache for their hurts and disappointments, but I'm so proud when they stand up tall.

I have finally accepted my need to have an odd job man. The

feeling of rising panic when anything goes wrong with the house was beginning to drive me mad. There's a limit to how much you can expect from sons, brothers or friends.

I have a great need to be more in control. My self-respect depends on being able to cope with minor emergencies. But I'm no Mrs Fixit, believe me, and changing a light globe is all the challenge I need.

Enter Kevin, recommended to me as honest, reliable and extremely competent. Suddenly, the creeper on the bathroom window is reaching heavenwards, firmly braced on wires that don't fall off or go rusty. The crooked shutter is straight and the blind back on the window again.

After talking to other single women about the problem of being hassled by servicemen, I took to keeping a file of plumbers, electricians, painters, carpet cleaners etc., who do a good job and don't charge the earth. Friends often ring for a name from my list. It's a very valuable document.

There's an art to relating to married friends when you're on your own. So often I hear single people complaining about how difficult it is to stay in touch with married friends. They say they no longer feel welcome and are hurt and confused by an apparent lack of closeness. Men, in particular, often find that their social structure collapses when they no longer have a wife. They feel condemned to a ghetto of other singles.

I was lucky in that several of my married friends picked up the threads without hesitation and helped me to weave a new pattern. I thought the pattern would be all lumpy and lopsided, and so it was for a time. Sometimes I wanted them to hold me close and say that I was fine. Other times, I wanted to stand apart and bleed and hurt like hell all by myself. That is the nature of grief.

Fortunately, most of my friends had the patience and innate kindness to put up with my moods. They had the courage to return over and over again and help me design a new pattern that would work for all of us. It takes a long time.

As you become more familiar with your new role, everyone relaxes and it gets easier. I still find that I'm not often included in 'married' dinner parties, but it doesn't bother me. I often invite a married couple to dinner on their own so that I have a chance to sit down and talk to them properly. I light the candles and do the flowers and serve food that needs no fuss.

Subscriptions to a concert or drama series help me to keep in touch on a regular basis. I invite friends who also have tickets for coffee at home afterwards. And all the time, I'm reaching out like a sweetpea looking for somewhere to climb towards the sun.

Meanwhile, the pattern I'm weaving is much clearer. It's not as lumpy as it used to be. I draw on clear, bright, sunny colours that give form to my days – which are now filled with a sense of wellbeing.

In contrast to his height and the size of his personality, Donald had an unusual reverence for things that were small. Like Sue, he melted before baby animals and birds and was an instant walkover with small children. So I guess it's not surprising that his favourite amongst all flowers was the Celmisia, or snow daisy, found on the rocky slopes of tall mountains.

I was invited to spend a summer weekend at a ski-lodge in the Mount Kosciusko National Park. It was a time of fierce heat and the place looked quite different from the snow-covered slopes of winter. I soon learnt that this group took their walking seriously. No slacking was allowed. Most of them had heavy boots and thick smelly socks to go with them.

So, it was with some trepidation that I set out on an

afternoon's 'walk'. We climbed a steep mountain where the air was thin and the view went on forever. Completely winded, I paused for a while to catch my breath. There, blooming all by itself in the midst of the alpine grasses, was a solitary snow daisy. Perhaps I was the only person in the world who saw that tiny flower. And yet, its life, though a brief day or two, seemed so special.

I often think about it and feel that we don't need to know why.

I have just watered the garden in the late afternoon sun. A thousand liquid diamonds are sparkling amongst the ferns. The good damp earth is fragrant with the freshness of growing plants.

I am humbled by the simple pleasures of life and grateful that I have lived long enough to be aware of them. There was a time when I lived for the future: the good things were always going to happen soon. Now, I know this isn't true. The gift of each new day is a miracle, which it's taken me a long time to understand.

If this were a painting instead of a story, the colours would be beautiful again now. The blues, pinks and greens of health and growth have returned in vibrant fullness. The pure gold of the sun glistens on a brilliant green landscape and the stars shine again in the night sky.

I still make cups of tea and thin bread and butter in the middle of the night. If I'm not sleepy, this little ceremony gives me great pleasure.

I don't lie awake because I'm unhappy or upset any more.

It's just that I'm older and don't seem to need as much sleep. But I don't mind. These solitary hours are thoughtful and restful, a time for quiet reflection or reading. I keep Jane Austen beside my bed and find that a few pages of her gentle prose and old-fashioned courtesy soon have me nodding off again. I listen to 'Music to keep the Days Apart' on the radio. It's comforting to know that over in the city, someone is playing music and talking to those of us who are still awake and listening.

The grandfather clock sounds loud and purposeful. Time is going places. It seems to say, 'Come on, Ann, there are things to be done and life to be lived. It's all happening out there. Get your coat on and go look at the stars.'

• *Sue's place for Christmas 1987* •

It's very early morning and I'm tucked up in bed with a cup of tea and a honey sandwich. A black cat nestles on the bed beside me. Everyone else is still asleep.

Rain is falling on the iron roof of the new verandah. I stand in the kitchen watching the multi-coloured bantams picking their way through the long grass and think how Donald would have loved it. The farmyard feeling of Sue's back garden, riotously overgrown, is somehow very comforting.

At dusk, the bantams arrange themselves in fluffy layers in the huge old wattle. The rooster trails his plumes like auburn and emerald streamers.

Mist enfolds the garden as darkness blurs the outline of familar things.

ALSO FROM McPHEE GRIBBLE/PENGUIN

A BIT OF A STRUGGLE

Jean McCaughey

Jean McCaughey's book looks at sixty-four families – low-income and better-off, single-parent, migrant, with unemployed members – living in one of Australia's worst areas of recession. Some have built up strong networks for coping and surviving to tide them over difficult times, while others teeter on the edge of disaster. These vivid, first-hand accounts of the joys and sorrows of family life range from the reassuring to the deeply disturbing – and there are no easy answers.

'This is a book for anyone concerned with the fabric of human relationship and development. It should be read by every thinking Australian who wonders about the future of family life.'

Age

ALSO FROM McPHEE GRIBBLE/PENGUIN

DEAR WRITER

Carmel Bird

Many people wanting to write do not know where to begin.

Carmel Bird, author of three books of fiction, has taught writing to a wide audience and understands the difficulties facing the new writer.

Dear Writer, a collection of letters to an aspiring author, speaks on the one hand about writer's block, about plots, about publishers, and, on the other hand, about the nature of fiction, offering the inspiration required for writing.

ALSO FROM McPHEE GRIBBLE/PENGUIN

A FOREIGN WIFE
Gillian Bouras

Gillian Bouras is an Australian married to a Greek. From the ambiguous position of a foreign wife, she writes of life in a Greek village. Her fellow villagers fondly regard her, the migrant in their midst, as something of a curiosity. They, in turn, are the source of both her admiration and her perplexity.

'Bouras writes about it all with great good sense and humour . . . This sharing of a family's life is very personal, generous and enjoyable.'

National Times

ALSO FROM McPHEE GRIBBLE/PENGUIN

YEAR ONE: A RECORD

John Tittensor

In June 1982, Jonathan and Emma Tittensor, aged nine and seven, were burnt to death in a house fire.

This is their father's description of the year that followed. A beautifully written account of the grieving process which is agonizing to read but leaves one grateful and humbled that such an experience has been shared.

ALSO FROM McPHEE GRIBBLE/PENGUIN

ANNIE STORIES

Doris Brett

Children often find it difficult to talk about things that are making them anxious.

Annie Stories are a way parents can help children feel comforted, supported, strengthened and understood.

Doris Brett incorporates, with the age-old practice of story-telling, simple but effective psychological techniques. Parents make up their own Annie Stories, changing Annie's name and background to one similar to their child's.

Annie Stories are easy to adapt and fun to tell. Better still, they really work.